An Econometric Model
of Postwar
STATE INDUSTRIAL DEVELOPMENT

by

Wilbur R. Thompson
and
John M. Mattila
Wayne State University

73909

DETROIT • WAYNE STATE UNIVERSITY PRESS • 1959

ACKNOWLEDGEMENTS

This is the report of the findings of a pilot study undertaken for the Michigan Department of Economic Development in connection with a broad and continuing program of analysis of the forces which influence state growth.

The parent program was initiated and guided by an advisory committee composed of Dr. Harold C. Taylor, Director of the W. E. Upjohn Institute for Community Research, Dr. Lloyd E. Fitzgerald, Dean of the College of Commerce and Finance, University of Detroit, Dr. Walter C. Folley, Dean of the School of Business Administration, Wayne State University, Dr. Russell A. Stevenson, Dean of the School of Business Administration, University of Michigan, and Dr. Herman J. Wyngarden, formerly Dean of the College of Business and Public Service, Michigan State University, and his successor, Dean Alfred L. Seelye. Dr. Taylor was chairman of the committee, Dr. Paul A. Herbert, Chief of the Research Division of the Michigan Department of Economic Development, was secretary, and Dr. Wilbur R. Thompson, Assistant Professor of Economics, Wayne State University, research director.

Financial support for the study came from a research grant to the Michigan Economic Development Commission made by The Michigan Bell Telephone Company, The Detroit Edison Company and The Michigan Consolidated Gas Company.

The W. E. Upjohn Institute of Community Research and the Michigan Department of Economic Development helped to finance the publication of the report.

PREFACE

In the late spring of 1957, a research advisory committee to the Michigan Economic Development Commission, anxious to anticipate the likely size and shape of Michigan's future economy, asked us to design a way of going about the business of forecasting industrial development at the state level. Since the need to frame better forecasts of the future is both clear and pressing, it would have been most convenient, expeditious, and economical to have proceeded directly to the matter of making predictions. But a hurried search failed to uncover either an established research design which was convincing in content or specific tools which were sharp enough to promise incisive analysis.

We could, of course, have been content to gather together some figures from the past on state employment in the various industries, plot the data on graph paper and with a straight edge—or perhaps a French curve— project the data boldly into the future. And this would not have been without value; but such an effort could be, and undoubtedly is being, done regularly (and probably just as well) by many private and public bodies whose fates are tied to the fortunes of the state. Considering then the primitive state of the art of regional forecasting and the natural forte of the University, the most logical and promising course of action seemed, to us, to be a broad, analytical one: to learn, first, more about the basic causes of the growth and decline of state economies. What we offer here is primarily a bit of *our* education as grist for *your* educated guesses.

Toward this end, we report here the results of a forty-eight-state multiple correlation and regression statistical analysis of employment growth in twenty varieties of manufacturing industry groups for the period 1947–54. Now, while our orientation has been more analytical than predictive, a rough and tentative outline of the future is implicit in our analyses— regression equations are, perforce, also estimating equations. But, then, if unwarranted generalization is, to the academic mind, the Scylla of research, excessive timidity is, to the practitioner, its Charybdis. We have ventured, therefore, to report employment estimating equations for thirteen (two-thirds) of the manufacturing industries studied, even while cautioning against too heavy reliance on any of them in their present first approximation forms. Still, there is much here that the planner-forecaster might well consider—consider, of course, in conjunction with the evidence and impressions he has gained elsewhere.

Further reformulation and retesting of these equations is both desirable and necessary: desirable to better fit the equations to the facts of industrial growth and necessary to reflect the temporal nature of the economic relationships outlined, defined as they are (and can only be) in terms of the recent past. So, to anticipate our conclusion: Nothing could be more gratuitous at this juncture than the customary disclaimer accompanied by the conventional structure that much remains to be done.

This study, with its nearly one thousand separate correlations, is truly a child of an advanced technology—the modern electronic computor, in particular. We must, accordingly, express our indebtedness to the Wayne State University Computing Center, and to Herschel Harrison, especially, for the efficiency with which this work was conducted. But the age of fully-automated statistical operations is not yet with us; therefore, our debt is even greater to Ronald M. Cronovich, Paul A. Gibson, Vicky A. Gross, Glenn C. Hague, Evan D. Macleod and James W. Thomson, research assistants, whose diligence and skill were far superior to that which we had any reason to expect. We wish also to acknowledge the contributions of Professor Harvey E. Brazer of the University of Michigan, who prepared certain key data series for us, and of Professors John B. Lansing of the University of Michigan and Victor E. Smith of Michigan State University, whose critical comments substantially improved the quality of the product.

Wilbur R. Thompson
John M. Mattila

December 1958

CONTENTS

I

A DESCRIPTION OF THE MODEL

The Scope: Space, Activities and Time

The first step in the formulation of our econometric model was to define the scope of the study in terms of space, activities and time. The state was selected as the appropriate unit of areal subdivision for two simple but compelling reasons. First, a much richer supply of economic data is available at the state level than for any other regional subdivision of the country and, second, while the state is seldom a natural economic region, it remains a vital unit of public policy. And forty-eight states constitute enough observations for statistical significance and manipulative convenience at this early stage of comparative analysis. All of which, of course, does not deny that further areal disaggregation would be well rewarding, probably even rating a priority over further industrial disaggregation.[1]

The model is limited to manufacturing industries, again partly for reasons of data availability. The federal government collects and tabulates manufacturing data in a form which allows comparisons to be made between states at a point of time (cross-section analysis) and for a given state through time (time-series analysis). But more than just the wealth of data, manufacturing industries account for the largest collection of jobs that are critical in the process of industrial development. "Critical" in the sense that manufacturing activity is usually basic in nature, that is, the products are sold in markets outside of the local economy and, hence, generate a stream of net income for the community—the export industries. (The basic industries are the region's breadwinners as distinct from the local-service industries, such as electric power and retail trade, which perform the vital but less dynamic housekeeping jobs.) This is not to say that all manufacturing activity is basic nor that only manufacturing activity is basic; just that this sector of the economy usually accounts for the lion's share of a region's vital exports. Moreover, manufacturing encompasses many, if not most, of the more locationally-mobile (potentially-migratory) industries

---

[1] That is to say, a point is reached, perhaps rather quickly, when the state should not be analyzed as a totality; the economic prospects of Detroit, Grand Rapids and Calumet, Michigan, are quite separable and distinct. And, too, a point is reached at which a dissection of the industry class, chemicals and allied products, would sharpen the analysis, although a preference is expressed here for regionalizing the state first.

1

and it is industrial migration that poses many of the critical problems of state industrial development.

A twenty-fold breakdown of manufacturing was adopted—the U. S. Bureau of the Census' (two-digit) major-industry-group classification. Some industrial disaggregation is necessary to expose the substantial variation within manufacturing; a finer breakdown than the one adopted was precluded by data limitations. True, the 1947 and the 1954 *Census of Manufactures* report data at the state level by very narrowly-defined industry classes but the interim *Annual Survey of Manufactures* (1949 to 1953) report manufacturing data at the state level for only the twenty major industry groups. Consequently, if a finer than twenty-fold breakdown had been adopted, postwar state industrial trends would have had to be estimated on the basis of two observations, a precarious business, especially in light of the fact that 1954 was a national recession year and national employment below that for 1947 was reported for many industries. Only by extracting our trend estimates from annual data could we avoid confusing a cyclical swing with a secular trend.

The time period selected was 1947–54. The base year, 1947, is the first postwar year for which the necessary Census data was available; fortunately, the year 1947 has the virtue of following long enough after the war to avoid reflecting the more marked war-wrought distortions in national-regional industrial structures but is still early enough in the postwar period to maximize the time period under observation. Finally, the year 1954 was the most recent for which data were available at the time of the data processing.

The Dependent Variables

An appropriate index of industrial development became the first requirement. A good case can be made for a number of measures: income, value-added, employment. But income data was available by states for only the broadest of industrial categories, such as manufacturing, wholesale and retail trade, preventing, thereby, any but the most gross analyses of industrial trends; value-added by manufacture reflects changing prices and, therefore, any projections based on postwar trends would implicitly incorporate a forecast of further inflation at the 1947–54 rate or entail the work of deflating the various time series, a difficult and probably unnecessary involvement at this stage; and employment data suffer from the presence of a questionable "weighting" arrangement, that is, no distinction is drawn between the kinds of jobs won or lost in terms of the skill required or the value-productivity of the worker—a job is a job. A discourse on the relative merits of these various measures would be digressive and gratuitous at this juncture. Let it suffice to say that employment was chosen as the index of industrial development because good data were readily available and also because even the *sheer number* of jobs (any and all varieties) won or lost is an important index of community welfare. But, admittedly, a comparison and blending of the results obtained from the use of alternative measures of growth is an important matter warranting proper concern as soon as time and resources permit.

One further feature of the dependent variable deserves especial attention. Employment growth can be measured either by the number of employees gained or lost or by the relative increase or decrease in employment. Both absolute change and rate of change have merit as growth indexes and the preferred choice depends on the analytical context. In the present context, absolute change is preferred primarily because of the extremely wide range of bases from which the rate of growth must be measured. The dilemma posed is that a very small increase or decrease in the number of workers employed produces a very large relative increase or decrease in employment in the many non-industrialized states. (The movement of a single plant into one of the Plains or Mountain states could effect a seven-year employment increase of as much as a couple of hundred per cent in many of the industry groups.) And even if such changes were relatively infrequent, which they are not, it takes only a few random changes of that magnitude to distort the mathematical formulation of an industry growth pattern. Moreover, on the positive side, the primacy of the *number* of jobs gained or lost is hard to deny. From a planning standpoint, public or private, it is usually the *number* of jobs, houses, school desks, motor vehicles, machines and so forth which we expect to have, to have to supply, or to have to accommodate in the coming years that occupies our attention.

And so, primary emphasis is placed on the measurement of industrial growth and development in absolute terms—the burden of the first three chapters. Fortunately, however, the early press of time and resources was ultimately relaxed sufficiently to permit the addition of Chapter IV, in which a parallel, if slightly truncated, rate-of-growth analysis was pursued and integrated into the model. While this latter material afforded an opportunity to make critical comparisons and more certain judgments, it is still quite accurate to regard the absolute-growth model now under consideration as the main theme of this study, with the rate-of-growth analysis acting as a complementary variation thereon.

The dependent variables of the model—that which we are attempting to statistically explain—are, then, interstate differentials in employment growth, 1947–54, for the various manufacturing industries. The specific form of the variable is the *estimated average annual change in the number of workers employed*, derived, in general, by computing the slope of a least-squares trend line fitted to the data. To illustrate, the following time series of employment in fabricated metal products in the State of Michigan:

1947	1948	1949	1950	1951	1952	1953	1954
92,305	90,480	88,654	113,079	108,354	98,882	123,640	91,671

yields an average annual increase in employment of 2,230 for the period, 1947–54. Corresponding calculations were made for each of the following Census major industry groups for each of the forty-eight states and the District of Columbia:

Y_{20}: Food and kindred products
$_{21}$: Tobacco manufactures
$_{22}$: Textile-mill products
$_{23}$: Apparel and related products
$_{24}$: Lumber and products
$_{25}$: Furniture and fixtures
$_{26}$: Paper and allied products
$_{27}$: Printing and publishing industries
$_{28}$: Chemicals and allied products
$_{29}$: Petroleum and coal products
$_{30}$: Rubber products
$_{31}$: Leather and leather products
$_{32}$: Stone, clay, and glass products
$_{33}$: Primary metal industries
$_{34}$: Fabricated metal products
$_{35}$: Machinery, except electrical
$_{36}$: Electrical machinery
$_{37}$: Transportation equipment
$_{38}$: Instruments and related products
Y_{40}: All manufacturing
(Y_{39}: Miscellaneous manufacturing was omitted because so ambiguous a classification lacks the preciseness which would permit meaningful analysis.)

Estimates of the various industry trends, by states, is presented in full in Appendix A.

The Independent Variables

The independent variables of the model—the presumed determinants of interstate differentials in industrial growth—are divided into two major groups: variables expressed in a form *general* to all manufacturing industries and variables expressed in a form which renders them *specific* to particular manufacturing industries. This distinction becomes sharper if one contrasts the growth of state population (a potential stimulant to growth for any and all manufacturing) with the number of patents on internal combustion engines issued to state residents (a potential stimulant to growth largely confined to transportation-equipment manufacturing). The industry-general variables will be correlated with employment change for all twenty manufacturing classifications while the industry-specific variables will, of course, be correlated selectively with only the relevant industry.

Growth of the Local Market

Within the group of industry-general variables, five broad sub-groups can be distinguished. First a set of comprehensive state-market-growth indexes—demand factors—were formulated:

X_1: Average annual change in state population, 1940–47.

X_2: Average annual change in state personal income, 1940–47.

X_3: Average annual change in state personal income, 1945–48.

The first two variables above, population growth (X_1) and personal income growth (X_2) represent alternative formulations of the expansion of the local (state) market during the seven years preceding the period of industrial change under study. The hypothesis here is that a state which is experiencing a rapid growth in population and/or income during a given period of time (1940–47) will be building a market for manufacturing products which will attract producers in the subsequent time period (1947–54). The rationale here is a familiar one: plant location in or near the product market to minimize transportation costs and facilitate contact with the customers. The choice of this particular time lag was admittedly quite arbitrary; further experimentation to establish the proper time lag should be a next order of business, especially in light of the fact that population and personal income proved to be the two variables most closely associated with state industrial development and excellent annual data are available. Some slight hedging on the score of the appropriate timing involved is evident in the alternative form (X_3) of the personal-income-change variable—average annual change for the *shorter, postwar* period, 1945–48.

Industrialization

A second industry-general group of variables have been loosely designated "industrialization" factors, namely:

X_4: Average annual change in total manufacturing employment, by states, 1939–47.

X_5: Expenditures for new plant and equipment in all manufacturing industries, by states, 1947.

X_6: Average annual number of patents and designs issued to residents, by states, 1946–48.

Looking first to the change in manufacturing employment in the preceding time period (X_4), the reasoning here is that an increase in manufacturing activity (employment) in an area should generate an increased local demand for various intermediate products, that is, should spawn various local suppliers to the original producers.[2] Especially, one would expect certain primary and capital goods industries (e.g., iron and steel, metal working, and machinery) to arise in response to a local growth in practically any and all types of manufacturing activity.

The second variable of the group, investment in new plant and equipment in the origin year (X_5), is of a somewhat different order than are most of the other variables in this model. Investment can hardly be regarded as a basic determinant of industrial development; rather it is more a reflection of some fortunate blend of favorable economic characteristics which invite financial exploitation; investment is the financial manifestation of a propitious time and a favorable environment. Still, since our objective is not only to understand better the forces which influence industrialization but also to forecast better the shape of the future, plant and equipment expenditures as a leading series or economic indicator may aid in accomplishing the latter, even if not the former, objective. Actually, in the present context, *aggregate* investment in *all manufacturing* facilities may be regarded as a broad, if gross, index of the degree of optimism imbuing local entrepreneurs or, better, the favor with which entrepreneurs everywhere view the area in question.

Of the three variables classified as indexes of industrialization, the last one is the most unconventional. Patent grants to residents, by states, 1946–48 (X_6), is introduced as a general measure of the vitality of local research and development. The reasoning here is that patent grants reflect research and development activity in both products and processes, which

---

[2] This is a kind of variation of the hallowed accelerator-multiplier theme. The acceleration principle ties increases in consumption to the resulting increase in investment (productive capacity) necessary to accommodate that higher level of consumption, while the multiplier effect connects this higher level of investment to a further increase in production, income and employment. While these linkages have usually been developed in a national-income, household-consumption context, a similar construction in a regional-employment, firm-consumption context is hypothesized here. Specifically, an increase in local manufacturing production and employment (X_4) requires an increased input (consumption) of plant, equipment and materials which in turn fosters an increase in the investment, production and employment of local (supplier) firms $(Y_{20\text{-}40})$.

in turn give rise to subsequent gains in production and employment. But, of course, a patent may be granted to a resident of a given state and that patentee may assign it to a firm in some other state, thus destroying the locational linkage between the creation of the idea and the gain in employment. And so, interstate differentials in patent grants will be looked upon less as direct instruments of job creation and more as a general index of the industrial creativity of the local populace. Patents, then, are cast in the dual role of indicators of possible competitive gains in technology accruing to the home state of the inventors and, more surely, indicators of the relative industrial proclivity and/or maturity of the populace of the home state.

State and Local Taxes

The third group of independent variables contains two forms of one of the hardiest perennials of state-growth analysis, the level of state and local taxes. There is no more frequently expressed fear in matters of interstate competition for business than the apprehension that firms are readily repelled by harsh tax treatment—and attracted by tax leniency. A number of investigations, most often by tax-study groups, have been conducted but, to date, very little in the way of conclusive evidence or even convincing argument has been adduced.[3] That which has been undertaken in this study is not intended as a full-dress analysis of taxes and location; rather the objective here is the much more modest one of merely testing the statistical association of interstate differentials in tax levels and industrial growth.

The level of state and local taxes is expressed in two distinct forms:

X_7: State and local taxes as a per cent of state personal income, by states, 1953.

X_8: Estimated state and local taxes paid by non-agricultural business per employee, by states, 1953.

The first form of the tax variable is probably the most conventional form of representing the tax load. The proportion of state personal income exacted by state and local governments (X_7) should probably be considered in conjunction with the value of the tax-financed government

---

[3] The explanation of the lack of convincing progress in this field of study is probably largely due to the difficulty of formulating incisive hypotheses in a testable form; this in turn is a manifestation of some combination of: (1) an uneasy theory of tax shifting and incidence, (2) lack of selective tax data, (3) uncertainty about the role of taxes as a business cost and locational factor, and (4) the difficulty of evaluating the at least partially-counterbalancing, tax-financed government services to business.

services returned to business—some *quid pro quo* exists. But in the absence of such data—or even criteria—tax payments will be treated as a total loss to business, at least as a first approximation.

But business firms probably do not avoid states or localities which pluck someone else's feathers. So, to be more incisive, an attempt was made to separate out those taxes which business pays and to relate them to some suitable common denominator. Thus, the second form of the tax variable becomes state and local business-taxes per employee (X_8). The taxes allocated to business were: various business license taxes (such as the corporate capital stock and annual franchise taxes), state corporate net income taxes and that portion of the state and local property taxes which were estimated to fall on non-agricultural business. The aggregate of these taxes was then divided by non-agricultural employment to yield a measure of tax load which would more precisely define the average burden which business must bear as the price of locating in a given state.

Ideally, the indexes of interstate tax levels should apply to the year 1947, the origin of the growth period under study, but state-by-state estimates of local government revenue are available only for the years 1942 and 1953, with the latter year the better choice for our purposes. The validity of the tax analyses rest, then, on the assumption that interstate tax differentials are relatively stable and that the *relative* position of a state probably would not have changed appreciably between 1947 and 1953. This assumption is probably much more critical to the accuracy of the tax analyses than any across-the-board tax increases which may have transpired during this period. (A general increase in state and local tax levels since 1947 could, however, have transformed taxes into a currently more influential locational factor, even if most states have held their relative positions through the years.)

Labor Market Characteristics

The fourth group of independent variables may be broadly designated as labor market characteristics, specifically:

X_9:   Average hourly earnings in manufacturing industries, by states, 1949.
X_{10}:   Estimated trade union membership as a per cent of non-agricultural employment, by states, 1947.

The first of the two variables, average hourly earnings (X_9), is an approximation of the regional wage rate. And, presumably, low wage rates tend to attract industry and stimulate employment growth while high wage rates tend to repel industry and dampen growth. One obvious shortcoming of our index is that average hourly earnings will exceed the average wage rate to the extent that the standard work-week is exceeded and overtime pay rates take effect. But this is probably not too serious because, while the year 1949 was chosen principally because it is the earliest year for which the Bureau of Labor Statistics data are available (1947, the origin year of the dependent variable, would have been preferable), the year 1949 has the virtue, as a wage-rate index, of being a period in which the standard work-week was seldom exceeded—a year of national recession. Average hourly earnings are not to be confused with labor costs; a regional labor cost index could be derived from the ratio of the regional wage rate to some interregional productivity index, which latter measure is, of course, unobtainable. And, in further limitation, relative wage rates are probably more often a *consequence of previous* rather than a *cause of future* inter-regional differentials in industrial development. But, even so, the interest in any association which may be found between comparative wage rates and employment change is such as to merit its inclusion.

The second of the two labor market variables, roughly, the per cent of the labor force organized (X_{10}), was chosen to test the often-expressed claim that firms flee or at least attempt to avoid unionized labor markets. Analogous to wage-rate differentials, the pervasiveness of unionism is probably more a consequence of earlier industrialization than a deterrent to further industrial development. But, again, intense private and public concern on this score supports the incorporation of a unionization variable in our model.[4]

Educational Levels and Facilities

The fifth group of independent variables consists of various expressions of the local educational level and facilities. Precisely, the three indexes adopted are:

X_{11}: Median years of school completed by persons twenty-five years old, and over, by states, 1950.

X_{12}: Number of persons twenty-five years old and over who have completed four or more years of college, by states, 1950.

X_{13}: Total staff, institutions of higher education, by states, 1947–48.

[4] Ideally, some complementary measure of industrial harmony or union-management maturity deserves consideration. An approximation to such a measure has recently become available: the Bureau of Labor Statistics' annual series on the per cent of estimated working days lost due to work stoppages. But the earliest year for which these data are available is 1952 and the data are so erratic that at least a three-year average would be needed to produce an index with any reasonable degree of stability. This would extend the relevant time period to 1952–54, the close of the growth period under consideration, rendering the variable of questionable value in either an analytical or predictive role. But future recourse to the idleness ratio holds promise, especially after enough of a time series has accumulated to appraise its trustworthiness (stability) as a regional indicator of industrial peace.

The first of the three, median school years completed, is obviously a measure of the level of mass education. It is the closest of the three to the concept of the skill-of-the-local-labor force—one of the most commonly mentioned locational factors, especially in surveys of manufacturers on factors affecting their locational decisions. Formal schooling is not, of course, synonymous with technical skill, although surely some (direct) relationship exists between general education and vocational competence. Unfortunately, a more direct measure of the quality of the local labor force is not available.[5] So in the absence of any direct quantification of technical skills, an index of the level of general education appears to be the broadest and most basic formulation of the concept of labor force quality that is now feasible.

An alternative expression of the character of the human resources of the state is attempted in the second variable of this group, the number of persons with four or more years of college (X_{12}). This is a rough approximation of the supply of very-highly-skilled and professionally-trained workers. Perhaps the form of this variable deserves some comment. The variable is expressed in an *absolute* form—as the number rather than the per cent of the population who have completed four or more years of college—because it was chosen to express a supply condition in our market equations. Contrast the case of Arizona, which in 1950 had 7.4 per cent of her adult population with four or more years of college, with that of Michigan, with only 5.3 per cent in a similar situation; but Arizona could supply only about 30,000 persons with a college education, compared to Michigan's supply of 194,000. Clearly, then, as a supply variable with which to explain the *absolute* change in various kinds of manufacturing employment, the *number* of college-educated persons is most appropriate. (A relative form of the variable, for example, per cent of the labor force who are college-trained, might have some relevance on the demand side, perhaps as an index of the attractiveness of the community as a living place.) Once more, the choice of the year (1950) for both X_{11} and X_{12} is justified by an even less satisfactory alternative (1940).

The third education variable, roughly, the supply of college faculty (X_{13}), is a variation on the immediately preceding variable. Here, it is the availability of educational facilities rather than educated manpower which

[5] Alternatives such as the per cent of the labor force classified as professional, technical, and kindred workers and/or craftsmen, foremen, and kindred workers (in contrast to operatives) might have been selected from the *Population Census*. But the weakness of this latter construction is that an occupational distribution of the labor force reflects, more than determines, industrial development. (That is to say, areas possessing industries with skilled labor requirements show occupational structures with a high per cent of skilled labor—a near tautology.)

has been quantified. The superiority of using college staff rather than some alternative measure of educational facilities, such as size or value of physical plant, is quite easily defended. If a state's institutions of higher education have any direct bearing on its rate of economic progress, it almost surely would be ascribable to the supply of personnel and not the amount of bricks and mortar put in place. Although it may well be that some more selective measure of higher-educational resources would have been preferable—the size of the engineering and natural science faculties rather than all faculty, for example—but if such information exists, it has not yet been uncovered.

Industry-specific Variables

Three variables have been added (in forty-seven variations) in a form which tailors them to particular industries, namely:

X_{14-20}: Average annual number of selected patents, by industry, issued to residents, by states, 1947–48.

X_{21-40}: Expenditures, by industry, for new plant and equipment, by states, 1947.

X_{41-60}: Employment, by industry, by states, 1947.

The first of these variables, selected patent grants, is presented for only seven of the twenty major industry groups:

Chemicals (X_{14})   Machinery, except electrical (X_{18})

Stone, clay, and glass (X_{15})   Transportation equipment (X_{19})

Primary metals (X_{16})   Instruments (X_{20})

Fabricated metals (X_{17})

Only seven sets of industry-specific patent grants are included due to the difficulty of assembling the data from primary sources; no geographic distribution of patent grants by patent classes has been compiled either by the U. S. Patent Office or by any other governmental agency. (Our data was painstakingly assembled from random, chronological entries in the *Official Gazette of the Patent Office*, a weekly publication.) The number of patent classes associated with a given industry group varied from seven in the case of the instrument industry (optics, photography, geometrical instruments, time-controlling mechanisms, surgery, dentistry, and artificial body members) to only one in the case of the transportation equipment industry (internal combustion engines).

The number of patent classes employed to characterize a given industry group was governed by both the number of patent classes which could be identified as belonging to a particular industry group and the number of patents granted in those classes in a given time period. The problem of identification and classification stems from the fact that patents are largely classified by process while industries are classified by product. The dilemma arises when processes cross product boundaries. For example, abrading (patent class ≠ 51) was associated with stone, clay and glass manufacturing (Y_{32}), which includes the sub-group abrasives. But many such patents might have an equal or even greater impact on, say, fabricated metals (Y_{34}) or instruments (Y_{38}), especially optical instruments. A further constraint is that a class such as internal combustion engines is so comprehensive and the frequency of patent grants is so great that merely to tabulate the data for this single class for two years was a laborious task (385 patents).

A fundamental distinction between the seven, industry-specific patent variables $(X_{14\text{-}20})$ and the one industry-general patent variable (X_6) discussed earlier is that each of the seven variables is introduced as an index of the potential employment gain which may accrue to a state due to the discovery of a new process or product by a local inhabitant—literally, an index of potential new jobs. In contrast, the industry-general variable (X_6) was rationalized more as an overall index of the technological creativity of the local populace—a kind of industrial-cultural index.

The second set of industry-specific variables, plant and equipment expenditures, by industry, 1947 $(X_{21\text{-}40})$, is a disaggregation of the same data introduced above as a general variable (X_5). Precisely stated, X_{21} is plant and equipment expenditures in food and kindred products manufacturing in 1947 and X_{22} is similar data for tobacco manufactures and so forth. But more than this, in its general form, investment was cast in the role of an overall measure of business optimism about the future prospects of the local economy, applicable to (and potentially explanatory of) employment trends in *any* of the major industry groups. Now investment is being offered as a specific supply variable; investment in physical facilities in an area is, normally, the concomitant and harbinger of increased production and employment in that area. Again, even though investment is not a causal factor in area development, it may prove to be a good leading series and have value for forecasting purposes.

Finally, the third set of industry-specific variables, employment in the various industries in 1947 $(X_{41\text{-}60})$, is both novel and obvious. It is certainly reasonable to expect that the amount of employment in a given industry at the beginning of a period of time is associated with the *absolute* amount of employment change in that industry during the succeeding time period. Obviously, Ohio could gain or lose a large number of machinery workers during the next decade much more easily than could Minnesota, not to mention Utah. What is represented here is, loosely, a kind of locational inertia. The hypothesis is that, barring good reason for spatial rearrangement, industrial expansion (contraction) tends to take place at existing locations and in direct relation to their relative size.

II

A FIRST APPROXIMATION OF THE RELATIVE IMPORTANCE OF THE VARIOUS DETERMINANTS OF STATE INDUSTRIAL DEVELOPMENT

Correlation Analysis: The Methodology

With the theoretical framework of our econometric model of state industrial development now complete, the next step is to test empirically the validity of the many functional relationships that have been hypothesized. Following this, the ultimate goal will be to define statistically the nature and the degree of these functional relationships. The basic methodology adopted to accomplish this task is the familiar "correlation and regression analysis."[6]

As a beginning, all the relevant simple correlation coefficients were computed, thereby providing a general framework of reference within which narrower, more intensive industry analyses could be pursued. While the traditional coefficients of correlation are reported in the accompanying tables, the increasingly familiar coefficient of determination will be the medium of expression in the text. The latter is mathematically the square of the former; its virtue is that it quantifies the association between the two variables in terms that are easy to grasp. To illustrate, a correlation coefficient of .70 can be transformed into a coefficient of determination of .49 ($.70^2$), which in turn can be translated into the statement that 49 per cent of the variation in one of the variables is associated with the variation in the other variable. Or, for our purposes, 49 per cent of the change in the dependent variable ($Y_{20\text{-}40}$) is statistically explained (not

---

[6] The conventional .05 level of significance will be applied to simple correlation coefficients, which level (for forty-nine observations) requires a coefficient of .28 or more. That is to say, only coefficients of .28 or more will be regarded as being statistically significant—a coefficient of that level could have arisen due to pure chance (i.e., would be meaningless) with a probability of only five in one hundred. It follows from this, then, that only those forces which can influence interstate differentials in employment growth by 8 per cent or more ($.28^2$) can be identified with (95 per cent) confidence; a weak growth force—a 6 or 7 per cent factor, for example—can not be established with a sample of only forty-nine observations.

necessarily caused) by changes in the associated independent variable (X_{1-60}). This simplicity of interpretation heavily favors primary dependence on the coefficient of determination as the appropriate statistical device through which to express any insights we may gain into the determinants and processes of industrial development.

It is worth noting at the outset that these simple correlations are not the final objective of this study, although they constitute an indispensable step along the way and are of great interest in themselves. Eventually, they will be combined in an industry-by-industry, multi-variate analysis of regional patterns of development. And, eventually, we hope to derive estimating equations with predictive value.

Correlation Results: Bi-variate Analysis

Growth of the Local Market

The results of the correlation of the three state-market-growth variables with the estimated employment trends of the twenty manufacturing industries are presented in Table 1. Even a cursory review of the coefficients reveals that the personal-income-change variable covering the longer time period (X_2) exhibits a consistently closer correlation with the dependent variables than does X_3, the alternative form, with the shorter time-lead; all of the statistically significant, positive correlations are higher with X_2 than with X_3. Concentrating attention on X_1 and X_2 then, further study of the results reveals that the association between the growth of the local (state) market during the period 1940–47 and the growth of employment in the subsequent period, 1947–54 is much closer in the case of the durable goods industries (roughly Y_{32-38}) than for the non-durable goods industries (roughly Y_{20-31}). Paper (Y_{26}) and printing and publishing (Y_{27}) are the only two non-durables to show close correlations; in fact, the very low association of both population and income growth with subsequent employment growth in non-durables is quite surprising.

A possible, partial explanation of this phenomenon is that many of the non-durables are strongly natural resource oriented (for example, food, tobacco, lumber and petroleum) being, thereby, relatively unresponsive to the call of the big city markets—markets feeding on the recent population migration trends. Of interest also is the fact that the two atypical non-durable goods industries, paper and printing, are heavy fixed investment industries, resembling the durables in that respect. But, lest too gross generalizations be drawn, chemicals, petroleum, and rubber are also characterized by heavy fixed investment and they behave more like the light non-durable goods industries.

Table 1. *Coefficients of Correlation of Selected Measures of the Growth of the Local Market with Estimated Average Annual Change in Employment, 1947–1954, by States, by Major Industry Group**

		Correlated with		
		Average annual change in		
		State population 1940–47	State personal income	
			1940–47	1945–48
	Major industry group	(X_1)	(X_2)	(X_3)
Y_{20}:	Food & kindred products	.31	−.18	−.42
21:	Tobacco manufactures	−.09	−.24	−.23
22:	Textile-mill products	−.03	−.34	−.38
23:	Apparel & related products	.33	.02	−.23
24:	Lumber & related products	.32	.16	.10
25:	Furniture & fixtures	.39	.36	.20
26:	Paper & allied products	.69	.66	.50
27:	Printing & publishing	.66	.46	.26
28:	Chemicals & allied products	.33	.29	.22
29:	Petroleum & coal products	.17	.02	.01
30:	Rubber products	−.11	.05	.07
31:	Leather & leather products	−.08	−.54	−.68
32:	Stone, clay & glass products	.62	.46	.33
33:	Primary metal industries	.49	.71	.67
34:	Fabricated metal products	.80	.86	.74
35:	Machinery, except electrical	.57	.74	.71
36:	Electrical machinery	.58	.82	.76
37:	Transportation equipment	.88	.74	.53
38:	Instruments & related products	.56	.79	.73
Y_{40}:	All manufacturing	.90	.86	.68

* *Derived from data presented in Appendix A, Table A-1 and Appendix B, Table B-1.*

Still, on the whole, the correlations of both population and income change with subsequent change in employment growth are highly significant for about one-half of the industry groups and remarkably high for the aggregate of all manufacturing. About 81 per cent of the variation between states in employment growth in all manufacturing is associated (statistically explained) by corresponding interstate differentials in population growth in the preceding time period. And prior population growth explains 77 per cent of the interstate variation in the employment trends of the transportation industry, 64 per cent of the variation in the fabricated metal industry, 48 per cent in paper, 44 per cent in printing and publishing, and 38 per cent in stone, clay and glass.

Table 2. Coefficients of Correlation of Selected Measures of Industrialization with Estimated Average Annual Change in Employment, 1947–1954, by States, by Major Industry Group*

		Correlated with		
	Major industry group	Average annual change in employment in all mfg. industries, 1939-47 (X_4)	Expenditures for new plant & equipment by all mfg. industries, 1947 (X_5)	Average annual number of patents & designs issued to residents, 1946–48 (X_6)
Y_{20}:	Food & kindred products	$-.34$	$-.29$	$-.21$
$_{21}$:	Tobacco manufactures	$-.29$	$-.32$	$-.21$
$_{22}$:	Textile-mill products	$-.40$	$-.37$	$-.50$
$_{23}$:	Apparel & related products	$-.12$	$-.03$	$-.12$
$_{24}$:	Lumber & related products	$.08$	$.06$	$.18$
$_{25}$:	Furniture & fixtures	$.21$	$.32$	$.18$
$_{26}$:	Paper & allied products	$.55$	$.58$	$.50$
$_{27}$:	Printing & publishing	$.41$	$.50$	$.32$
$_{28}$:	Chemicals & allied products	$.26$	$.34$	$.11$
$_{29}$:	Petroleum & coal products	$.02$	$.16$	$-.09$
$_{30}$:	Rubber products	$-.06$	$-.10$	$.07$
$_{31}$:	Leather & leather products	$-.65$	$-.54$	$-.60$
$_{32}$:	Stone, clay & glass products	$.42$	$.46$	$.44$
$_{33}$:	Primary metal industries	$.70$	$.76$	$.58$
$_{34}$:	Fabricated metal products	$.76$	$.78$	$.76$
$_{35}$:	Machinery, except electrical	$.74$	$.73$	$.69$
$_{36}$:	Electrical machinery	$.78$	$.78$	$.84$
$_{37}$:	Transportation equipment	$.59$	$.62$	$.58$
$_{38}$:	Instruments & related products	$.76$	$.79$	$.82$
Y_{40}:	All manufacturing	$.73$	$.76$	$.70$

* Derived from data presented in Appendix A, Table A-1 and Appendix B, Table B-1.

Prior interstate differentials in personal income change are associated with 74 per cent of the variation in fabricated-metal employment growth; and from one-half to two-thirds of the employment growth in primary metals, electrical and non-electrical machinery, transportation equipment and instruments. None of the variables to follow shows correlations with the dependent variable so consistently high over so wide a range of industries as do these two growth-of-the-local-market indexes.

Industrialization

The results of the correlations using the three selected measures of industrialization are presented in Table 2. Again, the pattern is clear: the durable goods industries exhibit an unbroken string of statistically significant, positive coefficients. And continuing the pattern revealed by the market-growth variables, only paper and printing and publishing of the non-durables behave like the heavy durables. The coefficients of all three variables (X_{4-6}) tend to run at about the same level for each of the industries. (This suggests the likelihood that these three independent variables measure various facets of a common, integrated complex: the industrially-mature economy.)

Of especial interest is the high correlation between growth of all manufacturing (as measured by employment) over the period 1939–47 (X_4) and subsequent growth in various metal, machine and tool industries. The variable X_4 explains 50–60 per cent of the interstate differentials in employment growth in primary metals, fabricated metals, machinery, electrical machinery and instruments. This is quite in line with the rationale elicited to support the selection of this variable: a growth in manufacturing would be expected to stimulate, especially, the basic metal, machine and tool industries, the indispensable handmaidens to industrial development.

The sharp bifurcation of the all manufacturing investment (X_5) correlations along durable-non-durable lines reinforces this rapidly crystallizing dichotomy. But it is not so clear why total manufacturing investment leads employment growth in the durable good industries but not in the non-durables—if the aggregate investment variable is performing in character: as an index of entrepreneurial expectations for an area. Aggregate manufacturing investment figures should, it would seem, signal growth in both manufacturing sectors, unless, of course, the total is dominated by expenditures for durable goods facilities. But, the vague, popular impression that durable goods production is characterized by heavier fixed investment notwithstanding, plant and equipment expenditure figures for 1947 show that the twelve non-durable goods industries spent about 50 per cent more than did the seven durables, leaving investment per industry very nearly the same in both groups.

The durable goods industries do, however, tend to live more agglomeratively (see the Addendum to this chapter) and, therefore, the all manufacturing investment figure for a given area will, perhaps, tend to contain a relatively rich mixture of durable goods plant additions as against a tendency for the investment aggregate to contain *either* this *or* that kind of non-durable manufacturing facilities. That is to say, an unspecified aggregate of manufacturing investment in an area will tend to entail a more balanced expansion of plant facilities in a variety of *locationally-linked* metal, machinery and toolmaking activities, whereas the non-durable portion of that aggregate might well be for, say, chemical plant only. If this explanation is rejected as somewhat too tortured, the results of the all manufacturing investment (X_5) correlations are not easily interpreted.

The last of the three industrialization variables is X_6, total patent grants at the inception of the time period under study. The coefficients indicate that the durable goods industries are more closely associated, locationally, with the regional distribution of inventive activity than are the non-durables. The inference here would seem to be that the heavy producers goods industries utilize more complex techniques and need to live in closer contact with the inventor. But whether the industries draw (or spawn) inventors or inventors draw (or spawn) the industries is not clear. (Clearly, the technically gifted and technically trained migrate to New York and Chicago for expression and further training, but just as clearly, those same persons found industries in out of the way places, for example, Henry Ford and Detroit.) But, in any event, total patent grants appear to be a fairly good indicator of employment trends in such industry groups as electrical machinery (a 71 per cent association), instruments (67 per cent), fabricated metals (58 per cent) and machinery, excluding electrical (48 per cent). (The virtual lack of any association between the all-patent-grants index (X_6) and growth in chemicals is somewhat surprising, *a priori*; but note the result of the chemistry patents index correlation below—$X_{14} Y_{28}$).

State and Local Taxes

The outcome of the correlations between the level of state and local taxes and manufacturing employment growth (Table 3) will not come as a surprise to anyone familiar with the results of previous, more direct investigations of the effect of taxes on industry location. True, the coefficients linking state and local taxes as a per cent of income (X_7) with employment growth display the expected (negative) sign more often than not—an inverse relationship is generally hypothesized, that is, high taxes repel industry and dampen employment growth while low taxes attract industry and stimulate employment growth. But not one of the simple correlation coefficients is statistically significant (at the .05 level).

Turning to the second form of the tax variable, the results are even less impressive. One would expect state and local taxes *paid by business* per non-agricultural employee (X_8) to express the presumed repelling effect of high taxes more precisely than the grosser index of *all* state and local taxes (X_7), but this business-tailored form of the variable performs even more erratically by displaying a positive sign (direct relationship) more often

Table 3. *Coefficients of Correlation of Selected Measures of the Level of State and Local Taxes with Estimated Average Annual Change in Employment, 1947–1954, by States, by Major Industry Group**

	Major industry group	Correlated with	
		State & local taxes as a per cent of state personal income, 1953 (X_7)	State & local taxes paid by business per non-agricultural employee, 1953 (X_8)
Y_{20}:	Food & kindred products	.10	.01
21:	Tobacco manufactures	.11	−.06
22:	Textile-mill products	.08	−.26
23:	Apparel & related products	−.05	−.04
24:	Lumber & related products	.15	.17
25:	Furniture & fixtures	−.06	.07
26:	Paper & allied products	−.04	.11
27:	Printing & publishing	−.22	.13
28:	Chemicals & allied products	−.17	−.15
29:	Petroleum & coal products	−.23	−.19
30:	Rubber products	.04	−.01
31:	Leather & leather products	.25	.00
32:	Stone, clay, & glass products	−.08	.20
33:	Primary metal industries	−.25	.03
34:	Fabricated metal products	−.15	.15
35:	Machinery, except electrical	−.17	.17
36:	Electrical machinery	−.19	.28
37:	Transportation equipment	−.17	.16
38:	Instruments & related products	−.22	.27
Y_{40}:	All manufacturing	−.19	.18

* *Derived from data presented in Appendix A, Table A-1 and Appendix B, Table B-1.*

than not. Actually, these latter, positive coefficients are not overly surprising. Firms in northern states pay a higher tax per employee than do their southern counterparts, but they pay it out of a higher value added per employee with probably no more financial strain. Added to this is the fact that the northern states are more heavily populated and contain larger employments in most industries, especially the metal, machine and tool industries (where the positive coefficients are close to being statistically significant). Then, the fact that the high business-tax states grew faster in durable goods employment than their counterparts seems to be quite reasonable and conventional.

Thus, while tax differentials may influence the locational decisions of particular firms at certain times, no significant evidence was uncovered to connect state and local tax levels with *interstate* differentials in *absolute* employment growth within *broad* industry classes. The contribution here is that this is probably the first time that the tax variable has been applied to so many sub-groups of manufacturing in so precise a form as the latter of the two indexes (X_8).

The general inference here is that high taxes are associated with an economic environment which provides the ability to pay them—or, perhaps, more accurately, an economic environment which exacts them as the price of the social costs of industrial maturity, that is, as the price of superior schools, highways, protection, public administration, etc. Now it *may* be that further disaggregation of industry would produce more narrowly-defined industries which do exhibit significant tax sensitivity, and there is an even greater possibility that an analysis of *local* tax differentials would reveal patterns of *intra*-state industrial migration. But, again, this does not purport to be a definitive tax study; it is, rather, a search for factors which will help to explain (and forecast) state growth patterns. And the relative level of state and local taxes offers, thus far, little promise.

Labor Market Characteristics

The coefficients derived from correlating the two labor market variables with employment growth appear in Table 4. Average hourly earnings (X_9) exhibit a mixed pattern of association with the dependent variables, eight negative and twelve positive correlations. An inverse association is, of course, the presumed relationship between wage rates and employment growth—low wage rates attract industry and spur employment growth and the reverse. And there is some slight evidence of this effect among the light non-durables, such as apparel, wherein 15 per cent of the variance is explained by wage rate differentials, and also in food, furniture, leather and (more surprisingly) primary metals, wherein about 7 per cent of the variance is so explained. But, conversely, the durable goods industries (except primary metals) show a slightly higher *positive* correlation with wage rates (around 10–14 per cent association). Lumber exhibits the only impressive amount of positive association, 34 per cent. Positive correlations probably do not reflect any direct line of causation; it would be difficult to accept high wage rates as a determinant of employment growth, *per se*. Surely, high wage rates produce high incomes, and the latter make for a good local market which in turn attracts and nurtures area industrial development (as is strongly suggested by Table 1). But high wage rates probably do not *effect future* progress so much as they *reflect prior* progress.

Table 4. *Coefficients of Correlation of Selected Measures of State Labor Force Characteristics with Estimated Average Annual Change in Employment, 1947–1954, by States, by Major Industry Group**

		Correlated with	
	Major industry group	Average hourly earnings in manufacturing industries, 1949 (X_9)	Estimated trade union membership as a per cent of non-agricultural employment, 1947 (X_{10})
Y_{20}:	Food & kindred products	−.28	−.40
21:	Tobacco manufactures	.12	.13
22:	Textile-mill products	−.17	−.26
23:	Apparel & related products	−.39	−.31
24:	Lumber & related products	.58	.45
25:	Furniture & fixtures	−.28	−.22
26:	Paper & allied products	.02	.21
27:	Printing & publishing	.13	.11
28:	Chemicals & allied products	−.07	.02
29:	Petroleum & coal products	.03	−.03
30:	Rubber products	−.08	−.10
31:	Leather & leather products	−.28	−.39
32:	Stone, clay & glass products	.16	−.06
33:	Primary metal industries	−.27	.34
34:	Fabricated metal products	.32	.28
35:	Machinery, except electrical	.38	.27
36:	Electrical machinery	.33	.34
37:	Transportation equipment	.36	.25
38:	Instruments & related products	.30	.32
Y_{40}:	All manufacturing	.33	.28

* *Derived from data presented in Appendix A, Table A-1 and Appendix B, Table B-1.*

The second labor market variable, per cent of the labor force unionized (X_{10}), behaves more in accordance with popular expectations. Employment growth in the more mobile industries with the lesser skill requirements, namely, food, leather, and apparel, exhibits a statistically significant (but still very modest) inverse relation with the degree of unionization; the coefficients for textiles and furniture fall just short of the .05 level of statistical significance but still suggest the possibility of some slight influence of a similar nature. These are the very industries one would have selected, *a priori*, as the most union-shy, that is, industries most likely to flee (or at least avoid) unions. (In fact, some sub-groups of these industries, shoes, for example, contain classic cases of union-induced flight.) But some measure of restraint is necessary here because in no case does the amount of union-explained variance exceed 16 per cent of the total variance to be explained.

The *positive* coefficients derived from the durable goods industries run along at a similar, modest level of significance, with only a 6 to 12 per cent direct association between degree of unionization and employment growth. The rational here may be that these industries have long been organized and have adjusted to the institution of collective bargaining and, with their heavy fixed investment (*locationally* as well as functionally fixed) and intensive skill requirements, they are relatively immobile, even if escape were possible. Consequently, employment growth in durable goods is taking place in the heavily unionized areas more often than not. (The high positive correlation in lumber is probably accidental and irrelevant—lumbering shifted from the non-union South to the heavily-unionized Pacific Northwest probably primarily in response to forest-resource changes.)

Educational Levels and Facilities

The correlation coefficients of the last group of general variables are presented in Table 5. The first of the three education variables, median school years completed by persons twenty-five years old and over (X_{11}), displays a set of surprisingly low coefficients. Employment growth in only one of the twenty industry groups (lumber) is significantly associated with this index of the level of mass education. While it is much too early to write off the average level of formal education of the labor force as a determinant of state industrial development, the results at least justify a healthy scepticism with respect to the potential usefulness of *this index* (or probably any minor modification thereof) in an explanatory or predictive role.

In sharp contrast, the number of college educated persons (X_{12}), exhibits a moderate to very high positive correlation with all durable goods industries, with a median explained variance of about 50 per cent. This compares favorably even with such strong variables as population (X_1) and income (X_2) growth. And, again, it is paper and printing from among the non-durables that behave in a fashion analogous to the durables.[7] The

[7] But while the higher coefficients for X_{12} indicate that this variable rather than X_{11} is likely to be of value in the employment forecasting attempted below, to infer from this that the supply of college graduates (X_{12}) is more critical to industrial development than is the overall level of education (X_{11}) is completely unwarranted. Since the more heavily populated states will ordinarily possess a greater number of college graduates (and college faculty X_{13}) and since these same states will ordinarily gain a greater number of workers—due to sheer size and inertia if nothing else—a

supply of college educated personnel is negatively correlated with employment growth in the leather and textile industries to a surprising degree. This may be quite meaningful. If areas which have a large number of highly trained persons attract those industries with higher skill requirements, and these latter pay higher wages, even for the more ordinary tasks, then the competition in the labor market would become too tough for the simpler skill industries forcing them to abandon the educated labor markets. (The surprisingly low coefficient for chemicals reminds us that the chemical industry has behaved quite independently throughout these general variable analyses.)

Finally, the correlation coefficients of the last of the general variables, roughly, college faculty (X_{13}), parallels the immediately preceding variable so closely (a correlation of .98 between the two) that one or the other is, in large measure, redundant. The number of college trained persons, however, has a slight edge over the number of college faculty members in closeness of fit. But the role of higher education in industrial development will probably not be fully revealed until some refinement of the growth index is attempted—presently, a job is a job. If, in place of total employment, the number of high-wage jobs or value added per worker of per-capita state income or some other similar measure of productivity were adopted as the dependent variable, a closer correlation between higher education and state economic development might well be recorded.

Industry-specific Variables

Finally, the three variables which were expressed in variations tailoring them to each major industry group remain to be considered. The relevant coefficients are set forth in Table 6. The first of these three, *selective patent grants* ($X_{14\text{-}20}$), exhibits the expected positive correlation and reaches

---

strong bias toward positive correlation is inherent in the X_{12} and X_{13} correlations. On the other hand, no such size-with-size positive correlation bias characterizes the X_{11} correlations; median school years completed is free from this pro-bigness bias; there is no reason, prima facie, why the median should be higher for New York than for Rhode Island.

In further argument, the *full adult population* (twenty-five years old and over) was correlated with employment growth in the various manufacturing industries; the coefficients which resulted are only a shade below those recorded for X_{12}. Specifically, the simple correlation coefficient linking all manufacturing employment growth with the full adult population of the various states is .79, as against .84 for college graduates, and the average of the coefficients in the seven durable goods industries is .69, as against .71 for college graduates. Thus, when measured against a variable which incorporates a similar positive correlation bias, the higher education effect is deflated to modest proportions. We are indebted to Professor Victor E. Smith of Michigan State University for pointing out the necessity for this caution in interpreting the results of these education correlations. (Size-with-size and other implicit biases in our model are discussed at some length in Chapter IV.)

*Table 5. Coefficients of Correlation of Selected Measures of State Educational Levels and Facilities with Estimated Average Annual Change in Employment, 1947–1954, by States, by Major Industry Group**

	Correlated with		
Major industry group	Median years of school completed by persons 25 years old & over, 1950 (X_{11})	Number of persons 25 years old & over who have completed 4 or more years of college, 1950 (X_{12})	Total staff, institutions of higher edcuation, 1947–1948 (X_{13})
Y_{20}: Food & kindred products	− .05	− .15	− .30
21: Tobacco manufactures	.22	− .24	− .25
22: Textile-mill products	− .19	− .40	− .13
23: Apparel & related products	− .27	.04	− .02
24: Lumber & related products	.54	.17	.10
25: Furniture & fixtures	− .20	.36	.35
26: Paper & allied products	− .13	.63	.58
27: Printing & publishing	.05	.43	.34
28: Chemicals & allied products	− .24	.24	.24
29: Petroleum & coal products	− .12	− .06	− .09
30: Rubber products	.01	.12	.19
31: Leather & leather products	.10	− .52	− .60
32: Stone, clay & glass products	.13	.44	.35
33: Primary metal industries	.07	.67	.68
34: Fabricated metal products	.13	.82	.74
35: Machinery, except electrical	.10	.70	.65
36: Electrical machinery	.14	.84	.82
37: Transportation equipment	.24	.71	.63
38: Instruments & related products	.08	.78	.72
Y_{40}: All manufacturing	.13	.84	.76

* *Derived from data presented in Appendix A, Table A-1 and Appendix B, Table B-1.*

about the same height as did the *general* patent grant variable (X_6). But there is considerable diversity in their respective performances between industries; the industry-specific form exhibits a much higher correlation coefficient in chemicals (raising the explained variance from nothing to 18 per cent), a moderately higher coefficient in primary metals (raising the explained variance from 34 to 44 per cent) and a slight edge in machinery (from 48 to 50 per cent). It is worth noting at this juncture that the chemistry patent index (X_{14}) was the broadest in scope and included the largest sample of patents—was probably the best—and that the primary metal-

Table 6. Coefficients of Correlation of Selected Measures of Development Specific to a Particular Industry with Estimated Average Annual Change in Employment in that Industry, 1947–54, by States, by Major Industry Group*

	Correlated with		
Major industry group	Average annual number of selected patents issued to state residents, 1947–8 (X_{14-20})	Expenditures, by industry, for plant and equipment, 1947 (X_{21-40})	Employment, by industry, 1947 (X_{41-60})
Y_{20}: Food & kindred products		− .21	.67
21: Tobacco manufactures		− .73	− .86
22: Textile-mill products		− .17	− .27
23: Apparel & related products		.02	− .11
24: Lumber & related products		.57	.07
25: Furniture & fixtures		.33	.32
26: Paper & allied products		.69	.51
27: Printing & publishing		.36	.10
28: Chemicals & allied products	.42	.43	.28
29: Petroleum & coal products		.39	.48
30: Rubber products		− .34	− .42
31: Leather & leather products		− .50	− .73
32: Stone, clay & glass products	.39	.37	.21
33: Primary metal industries	.66	.78	.77
34: Fabricated metal products	.73	.72	.65
35: Machinery, except electrical	.71	.59	.65
36: Electrical machinery		.22	.80
37: Transportation equipment	.54	.33	.48
38: Instruments & related products	.69	.51	.59
Y_{40}: All manufacturing		.76	.65

* *Derived from data presented in Appendix A, Table A-1 and Appendix C, Tables C-1, C-2 and C-3.*

related patent series is judged to be the next most representative collection of industry associated inventions. (A review of the patent class mixes as set forth in Appendix C will corroborate this judgment.) These results suggest that a selective patent grants index holds more promise than is now apparent or realizable—with further refinement.

Oddly, investment is less closely associated with employment growth in the heavy durables in its industry-specific form (X_{21-40}) than it is in its general form (X_5). Neither form proves to be of much value in explaining the employment growth of two-thirds of the non-durable goods industries. But the industry-specific form of the investment variable does provide a much better explanation of the variation in employment growth in paper, lumber, and petroleum. On the basis of 1947 new plant and equipment expenditure figures, 48 per cent of the interstate variation in the 1947–54 growth of manufacturing employment in the paper industry could have been predicted, 32 per cent in lumber, 18 per cent in chemicals and 15 per cent in petroleum. While well short of the spectacular in performance, these results suggest that the industry specific investment variable should occasionally play an important supporting role in employment forecasting, especially in the non-durable goods industries.

The third set of industry specific variables, employment in the various industry groups in 1947 ($X_{41\text{-}60}$), deserves special comment. *Positive* correlation expresses a relationship in which states with the greater amount of employment in a given industry (1947) added more or lost fewer workers in that industry (1947–54) than states with lesser employments. In contrast, *negative* correlation indicates a situation in which states with the larger industry employment gained less or lost more workers than smaller employment states.[8]

The strongest tendencies for the leading states to fatten their leads occurred in the durable goods industries with the exception of stone, clay and glass and with the tendency only moderate in transportation equipment. Among the non-durables, food and to a lesser degree paper and petroleum show a similar tendency toward locational inertia. All manufacturing also showed a regional tendency for the rich to get richer. A substantial reduction in the numerical lead of the dominant states is evident in tobacco and leather, with rubber exhibiting a modest tendency in the same direction. A generalized explanation of this pattern of industry behavior might be expressed as follows: Locational inertia seems to build

[8] But it does not follow from this that a positive correlation signifies increasing regional concentration of the industry, nor a negative correlation, regional dispersion. If a state with one-half of the total employment in a given industry added more workers than any other state but still less than one-half of the new workers, the correlation would be positive even though that state's *relative* share of the industry would be decreasing; if this state lost the most but still declined less than proportionately, a negative correlation would be consistent with the growing relative share of the dominant state. It is accurate only to draw inferences expressed in absolute terms, specifically:

(a) positive correlation indicates that the *absolute* leads of the larger employment states are widening, either because they are gaining more or losing less workers than the smaller employment states—faring better in number;

(b) negative correlation indicates that the *absolute* leads of the larger employment states are narrowing, either because they are gaining fewer or losing more workers than the smaller employment states—faring worse in number.

up more often than not and, quite expectedly, it appears to be most characteristic of industries with heavy, fixed investment and more complex technologies (for example, metals, machinery and tools plus paper and oil). These results suggest that employment in a given industry at the inception of the growth period ($X_{41\text{-}60}$) is closely enough associated with the subsequent average annual change in employment in that industry to merit careful consideration in the forecasting work to follow—at least for about half of the major industry groups.

ADDENDUM TO CHAPTER II

INTER-INDUSTRY LOCATIONAL LINKAGES IN STATE INDUSTRIAL DEVELOPMENT

An interesting and valuable by-product of this model is the matrix of coefficients of correlation between the various dependent variables. With very little extra effort or expense, a correlation analysis can be programmed for electronic computers which will match not only all the independent with all the dependent variables but also all the dependent variables with each other. These latter 190 correlation coefficients are set forth in the matrix of Table 7. Each of these coefficients measures the association of interstate differentials in the growth of employment in one major industry group with the corresponding variations in employment growth between states in the paired industry. For example, the correlation coefficient for leather (Y_{31}) and food (Y_{20}) is .56, that is, 31 per cent ($.56^2$) of the variations in employment growth in leather between states is associated with corresponding interstate variations in food employment growth. (Reflecting in part, perhaps, the by-product tie-in between meat packing and leather processing.) The full set of inter-industry correlations for any given industry can easily be compared by reading horizontally to the number 1 (the perfect correlation of an industry with itself) and then down the column under that number 1.

Close examination of the contents of Table 7 reveals a number of general patterns. Most notable is the high positive correlations in the employment growth between the various pairs of durable goods industries. From stone, clay and glass (Y_{32}) through instruments (Y_{38}), the inter-industry association among durables ranges from a low of 11 per cent (stone, clay and glass with primary metals) to a high of 64 per cent (electrical machinery with instruments), with a median association of 29 per cent. Within this group, fabricated metals displays the highest association with other durables (a median association of 51 per cent) and stone, clay and glass, the lowest (a median of 18 per cent). Fabricated metals appears, inferentially, to be a key industry in the development of a heavy industry complex, nearly all employment growth in the durable goods industries accompanies or is accompanied by (not to say, is caused by or causes) growth in fabricated metal employment. The association is quantitatively close and probably is also functionally linked, for example, customer-supplier relationships,

Table 7. *Coefficients of Correlation of Estimated Average Annual Change in Manufacturing Employment between the Various Census Major Industry Group, by States, 1947–54*

A: Non-durable goods industries
B: Non-durable goods with durable goods industries
C: Durable goods industries

	Food	Tobacco	Textiles	Apparel	Lumber	Furniture & fixtures	Paper	Printing & publishing	Chemicals	Petroleum	Rubber	Leather	Stone, clay & glass	Primary metals	Fabricated metals	Machinery, except electrical	Electrical machinery	Transportation equipment	Instruments	All manufacturing
Y_{20}: Food & kindred products	1																			
Y_{21}: Tobacco manufactures	.00	1																		
Y_{22}: Textile-mill products	.36	−.12	1																	
Y_{23}: Apparel & related products	.53	−.10	−.06	1																
Y_{24}: Lumber & related products	−.05	.22	−.10	−.23	1															
Y_{25}: Furniture & fixtures	.22	−.61	−.10	.52	.23	1														
Y_{26}: Paper & allied products	.22	−.10	−.09	.38	.06	.43	1													
Y_{27}: Printing & publishing	.34	−.25	−.01	.38	.07	.28	.52	1												
Y_{28}: Chemicals & related products	−.07	−.07	.16	.28	−.13	.18	.23	.32	1											
Y_{29}: Petroleum & coal products	.08	.07	.22	.09	−.30	−.03	.11	.31	.29	1										
Y_{30}: Rubber products	−.19	.04	−.37	.02	.02	.25	−.12	−.44	−.24	−.37	1									
Y_{31}: Leather & leather products	.56	.12	.20	.39	−.03	.16	−.19	.36	−.05	.11	−.04	1								
Y_{32}: Stone, clay & glass	.28	−.09	.11	.14	.11	.03	.44	.55	.24	.29	−.40	−.11	1							
Y_{33}: Primary metal industries	−.29	−.25	−.28	−.06	.11	.27	.38	.54	.32	.19	−.11	−.39	.33	1						
Y_{34}: Fabricated metal products	.07	−.15	−.10	.08	.25	.29	.68	.49	.23	.04	−.23	−.33	.66	.51	1					
Y_{35}: Machinery, except electrical	−.02	−.13	−.14	−.02	.07	.12	.49	.51	.25	.11	−.23	−.32	.45	.35	.75	1				
Y_{36}: Electrical machinery	−.19	−.15	−.58	.06	.30	.32	.49	.30	.13	−.17	.23	−.50	.41	.61	.70	.43	1			
Y_{37}: Transportation equipment	.16	−.04	−.04	.18	.34	.20	.58	.70	.25	.09	−.13	−.19	.62	.54	.78	.64	.59	1		
Y_{38}: Instruments & related products	−.05	−.30	−.51	.16	.18	.47	.55	.45	.14	−.01	−.01	−.32	.37	.54	.74	.61	.80	.51	1	
Y_{40}: All manufacturing	.14	−.18	−.06	.19	.30	.33	.70	.70	.35	.07	−.15	−.29	.65	.61	.88	.72	.69	.95	.65	1

Major industry group

joint products, common technologies and common service or skill requirements.

Of the many non-durable goods industries, only paper and printing are closely associated with the durable goods industries. The other three heavy fixed investment, non-durable goods industries, chemicals, petroleum and rubber, show no notable spatial linkage to the durables. And only a few isolated spatial linkages are evident among the non-durables themselves, notably: paper with printing (27 per cent association) and food with leather (31 per cent), both cited above, and apparel with food (28 per cent) and apparel with furniture (27 per cent). The first three of these four couplets reflect a close customer-supplier relationship, at least in part.

A number of significant negative correlations appear. The existence of an inverse relationship may be evidence either that the two industries seek diverse environments or that one tends to repel the other. This latter case may be exemplified by the series of rather high negative coefficients between food, textiles, leather and, perhaps even rubber, on the one hand, and the seven durable goods industries, on the other hand. This probably reflects, in large measure, a labor market incompatibility of these non-durables with the dominating durable goods industries—the former industries can rarely afford to meet the wage competition of the latter.

Although time limitations have precluded any intensive analysis of these many inter-industry growth linkages, Table 8 details the employment growth linkages between the major industry groups for the interested reader. All the inter-industry growth associations that are statistically significant at the .05 level (an association of 8 per cent or more in the present sample) are ranked by industry.

Without attempting to catalog the many possible uses of inter-industry growth linkages, two related possibilities readily suggest themselves. On the basis of the kinds of industries that are currently developing in a given area, information such as that presented in Tables 7 and 8 might be useful in predicting the likely accompanying (complementary) industrial developments. That is to say, metal manufacturing may attract machinery manufacturing (or vice-versa) and both may well repel textiles, leather and rubber manufacturing. Clearly, much remains to be done—especially with time series analysis—to establish the lines of causation or, at the very least, the chronological sequences involved.

Again, on the basis of the successful development of a given industry in the area (say, apparel), other industrial prospects may be considered by the "area industrial development commission" in the order of their likelihood of being compatible with current local industrial developments (beginning with, say, food and furniture). As guides for advertising and interviewing priorities these measures of inter-industry locational linkage offer considerable promise—but only after some further refinement.

Table 8. Coefficients of Determination of Estimated Average Annual Change in Employment in Each Major Industry Group with the Employment Change in Each Other Industry Group with Which it is Significantly Associated, by States, 1947–54

Major industry group	Percentage association of changes in employment, 1947–54
Y_{20}: FOOD & KINDRED PRODUCTS with:	
31: Leather & products	32
23: Apparel & related products	28
22: Textile mill products	13
27: Printing & publishing	11
32: Stone, clay & glass	8
Y_{21}: TOBACCO MANUFACTURES with:	
(No statistically significant correlation)	
Y_{22}: TEXTILE MILL PRODUCTS with:	
20: Food & kindred products	13
Y_{23}: APPAREL & RELATED PRODUCTS with:	
20: Food & kindred products	28
25: Furniture & fixtures	27
31: Leather & products	15
26: Paper & allied products	15
27: Printing & publishing	14
28: Chemicals & allied products	8
Y_{24}: LUMBER & PRODUCTS with:	
37: Transportation equipment	12
36: Electrical machinery	9
40: All manufacturing	9
Y_{25}: FURNITURE & FIXTURES with:	
23: Apparel & related products	27
38: Instruments & related products	22
26: Paper & allied products	19
40: All manufacturing	11
36: Electrical machinery	10
34: Fabricated metal products	9
27: Printing & publishing	8
Y_{26}: PAPER & ALLIED PRODUCTS with:	
40: All manufacturing	70
34: Fabricated metal products	46
37: Transportation equipment	34
38: Instruments & related products	30
27: Printing & publishing	27
35: Machinery, except electrical	24
36: Electrical machinery	24

Table 8—Continued

Major industry group	Percentage association of changes in employment, 1947–54
32: Stone, clay & glass products	20
25: Furniture & fixtures	19
23: Apparel & related products	15
33: Primary metal industries	14
Y_{27}: PRINTING & PUBLISHING with:	
40: All manufacturing	49
37: Transportation equipment	49
32: Stone, clay & glass products	30
33: Primary metal industries	29
26: Paper & allied products	27
35: Machinery, except electrical	26
34: Fabricated metal products	24
38: Instruments & related products	20
23: Apparel & related products	14
31: Leather & products	13
20: Food & kindred products	11
28: Chemicals & allied products	10
29: Petroleum & coal products	10
36: Electrical machinery	9
25: Furniture & fixtures	8
Y_{28}: CHEMICALS & ALLIED PRODUCTS with:	
40: All manufacturing	13
27: Printing & publishing	10
33: Primary metal industries	10
29: Petroleum & coal products	9
23: Apparel & related products	8
Y_{29}: PETROLEUM & COAL PRODUCTS with:	
27: Printing & publishing	10
28: Chemicals & allied products	9
32: Stone, clay & glass products	8
Y_{30}: RUBBER PRODUCTS (No statistically significant correlation)	
Y_{31}: LEATHER & LEATHER PRODUCTS with:	
20: Food & kindred products	32
23: Apparel & related products	15
27: Printing & publishing	13
Y_{32}: STONE, CLAY & GLASS PRODUCTS with:	
34: Fabricated metal products	44
40: All manufacturing	42
37: Transportation equipment	38

Table 8—Continued

Major industry group	Percentage association of changes in employment, 1947–54
27: Printing & publishing	30
35: Machinery, except electrical	20
26: Paper & allied products	20
36: Electrical machinery	17
38: Instruments & related products	14
33: Primary metal industries	11
29: Petroleum & coal products	8
20: Food & kindred products	8
Y_{33}: PRIMARY METAL INDUSTRIES with:	
40: All manufacturing	37
36: Electrical machinery	37
37: Transportation equipment	30
38: Instruments & related products	29
27: Printing & publishing	29
34: Fabricated metal products	26
26: Paper & allied products	14
35: Machinery, except electrical	12
32: Stone, clay & glass products	11
28: Chemicals & allied products	10
Y_{34}: FABRICATED METAL PRODUCTS with:	
40: All manufacturing	78
37: Transportation equipment	61
35: Machinery, except electrical	57
38: Instruments & related products	55
36: Electrical machinery	48
26: Paper & allied products	46
32: Stone, clay & glass products	44
33: Primary metal industries	26
27: Printing & publishing	24
25: Furniture & fixtures	9
Y_{35}: MACHINERY, EXCEPT ELECTRICAL with:	
34: Fabricated metal products	57
40: All manufacturing	52
37: Transportation equipment	41
38: Instruments & related products	37
27: Printing & publishing	26
26: Paper & allied products	24
32: Stone, clay & glass products	20
36: Electrical machinery	19
33: Primary metal industries	12
Y_{36}: ELECTRICAL MACHINERY with:	
38: Instruments & related products	63

Table 8—Concluded

Major industry group	Percentage association of changes in employment, 1947–54
34: Fabricated metal products	48
40: All manufacturing	48
33: Primary metal industries	37
37: Transportation equipment	35
26: Paper & allied products	24
35: Machinery, except electrical	19
32: Stone, clay & glass products	17
25: Furniture & fixtures	10
27: Printing & publishing	9
24: Lumber & products	9
Y_{37}: TRANSPORTATION EQUIPMENT with:	
40: All manufacturing	90
34: Fabricated metal products	61
27: Printing & publishing	49
35: Machinery, except electrical	41
32: Stone, clay & glass products	38
36: Electrical machinery	35
26: Paper & allied products	34
33: Primary metal industries	30
38: Instruments & related products	26
24: Lumber & products	12
Y_{38}: INSTRUMENTS & RELATED PRODUCTS with:	
36: Electrical machinery	63
34: Fabricated metal products	55
40: All manufacturing	43
35: Machinery, except electrical	37
26: Paper & allied products	30
33: Primary metal industries	29
37: Transportation equipment	26
25: Furniture & fixtures	22
27: Printing & publishing	20
32: Stone, clay & glass products	14
Y_{40}: ALL MANUFACTURING with:	
37: Transportation equipment	90
34: Fabricated metal products	78
35: Machinery, except electrical	52
27: Printing & publishing	49
26: Paper & allied products	49
36: Electrical machinery	48
38: Instruments & related products	43
32: Stone, clay & glass products	42
33: Primary metal industries	37
28: Chemicals & allied products	13
25: Furniture & fixtures	11
24: Lumber & products	9

III

A FIRST APPROXIMATION OF EMPLOYMENT ESTIMATING EQUATIONS FOR SELECTED MANUFACTURING INDUSTRIES

This study had its origins in the widely-felt need for some technique, tool or device with which state employment trends might be predicted. Forecasting is, admittedly, a hazardous undertaking, and the allowable margin for error should be generous. But plans presume forecasts and educated guesses are to be preferred over either wild guesses or the conventional straight-line projections. In short, this study is predicated on the belief that in the absence of a crystal ball there should be some better tool kit than mere graph paper and a ruler.

The methodology adopted here is a well-known and time-honored statistical technique: multiple correlation and regression analysis. But, due to its rather complicated computational character, it has been little used by the various private and public organizations who must make plans with an eye to trends in regional development. This statistical technique takes the simple correlation coefficients as the grist to be milled, manipulates them into various combinations and re-combinations, and ends up with that *set* of independent variables which is most closely associated with the dependent variable. And an equation is derived from which the value of the dependent variable can be estimated by inserting the values of the various independent variables into the formula. Moreover, it will be recalled that a continuing effort has been made to formulate and establish time leads in the independent variables. Not only is the model analytically stronger for this but, more relevant to our present purpose, if the independent variables apply to a given period (say, circa 1960) and the dependent variables to a later time (say, 1960–70), then a valuable predictive device has been fashioned.

Employment Estimating Equations for Selected Industries

Drawing on the statistical analysis above, we have derived estimating equations for thirteen of the twenty major industry groups.[9] These

---

[9] We have omitted estimating equations for the other seven major industry groups because the multi-variate analyses did not significantly improve the results of the simple correlations. Any results which might be reported would almost certainly be too tenuous to be useful and could even be misleading.

Table 9a. Coefficients of Correlation of Estimated Average Annual Change in Employment in Major Industry Groups, by States, 1947–1954, with Selected Determinants of State Economic Development

Selected determinants of economic development	Coefficients of Correlation			
	(Y_{20}) Food & kindred products	(Y_{21}) Tobacco manufactures	(Y_{22}) Textile-mill products	(Y_{23}) Apparel & related products

Growth of the local market

X_1: Average annual change in state population, 1940–47	.31	−.09	−.03	.33
X_2: Average annual change in state personal income, 1940–47	−.18	−.24	−.34	.02
X_3: Average annual change in state personal income, 1945–48	−.42	−.23	−.38	−.23

Industrialization

X_4: Average annual change in employment in all manufacturing industries, 1939–47	−.34	−.29	−.40	−.12
X_5: Expenditures for plant and equipment by all manufacturing industries, 1947	−.29	−.32	−.37	−.03
X_6: Average annual number of patents issued to state residents, 1946–48	−.21	−.21	−.50	−.12

State and local taxes

X_7: State and local taxes as a per cent of state personal income, 1953	.10	.11	.08	−.05
X_8: Estimated state and local taxes paid by business per non-agricultural employee, 1953	.01	−.06	−.26	−.04

Labor market characteristics

X_9: Average hourly earnings in manufacturing industries, 1949	−.28	.12	−.17	−.39
X_{10}: Estimated trade union membership as a per cent of non-agricultural employee, 1947	−.40	.13	−.26	−.31

Educational levels and facilities

X_{11}: Median years of school completed by persons twenty-five years old and over, 1950	−.05	.22	−.19	−.27

Table 9a (Continued)

	Coefficients of Correlation			
Selected determinants of economic development	(Y_{20}) Food & kindred products	(Y_{21}) Tobacco manufactures	(Y_{22}) Textile-mill products	(Y_{23}) Apparel & related products
X_{12}: Number of persons twenty-five years old and over who completed four years or more of college, 1950	$-.15$	$-.24$	$-.40$	$.04$
X_{13}: Total staff, institutions of higher education, 1947–48	$-.30$	$-.25$	$-.43$	$-.02$
Industry-specific variables				
X_{14-20}: Average annual number selected patents issued to state residents, 1947–48				
X_{21-40}: Expenditures for plant and equipment, by industry, 1947	$-.21$	$-.73$	$-.17$	$.02$
X_{41-60}: Employment, by industry, 1947	$.67$	$-.86$	$-.27$	$-.11$

equations are, however, to be regarded only as first approximations of the formulas which will best foretell the industrial employment future of a state. And, while some further refinement is possible even within the framework of the existing model, substantial improvement, the second approximation, awaits a basic reformulation of the model, incorporating the experiences of this and such other current studies as come to light.

Apparel and Related Products (Y_{23})

Turning first to the apparel industry, the various simple correlation coefficients which apply to that industry can be quickly reviewed by running down the fourth column of Table 9a. (Table 9 is a cross-classification of the data presented in Tables 1–6, arranged by industry groups rather than by groups of independent variables.) While none of the simple correlations are singly very impressive, some combination of two or more independent variables may effect an appreciable improvement. Of all the possible patterns of combination, a composite of the prior average annual population growth of the state (X_1) and the average hourly earnings in manufacturing in the state (X_9) produced the closest association with the dependent variable (average annual change in employment in apparel in that state). The simple correlation coefficients (.33 and $-.39$, respectively) combine to yield a multiple correlation coefficient of .58, thereby raising the explained variance from 15 per cent for X_9 alone and only 11 per cent for X_1 alone to 34 per cent for the two together, a very sizable jump but to a still rather modest level. The relevant estimating equation is:

$$Y_{23} = 2,526.3 + 4.83\ X_1 - 1,798\ X_9 \pm 529$$

That is to say the annual change in apparel employment in a given state in the coming period is estimated to be 2,526 workers *plus* 4.83 times the average annual change in population (in thousands) during the recent past *minus* 1,798 times the current average hourly earnings in manufacturing in that state. The actual number of workers added will fall within a range of plus or minus 529 workers of the predicted figure with a probability of about two out of three. The signs of the coefficients preceding the independent variables indicate the nature of the functional relationship; X_1 is positive, indicating that an increase in population tends to increase employment in apparel in the subsequent time period and the negative sign preceding X_9 indicates that high wage rates at the beginning of the period tend to dampen employment growth and low wage rates tend to stimulate employment in apparel. An analysis of the regression coefficients in standard units indicates that these two variables have roughly equal weight in the equation—are of equal importance.[10]

Lumber and Related Products (Y_{24})

The results of the multi-variate analysis of lumber manufacturing employment growth are reproduced here more for educational than analytical purposes. The two highest simple correlation coefficients registered for this industry group were those for average hourly earnings (X_9) and for investment in lumber manufacturing facilities (X_{25}), .58 and .59, respectively. While the latter expresses a reasonable functional relationship, that *high* wage rates should be a bellwether of rapid growth in lumber manufacturing employment (the correlation is positive) is not nearly so convincing. (Although the reverse, a statement to the effect that the lumbering centers

[10] When regression coefficients are expressed in standard units the relative contribution of each variable to the combined explained variance can be evaluated by directly comparing their numerical values. For example, referring to Table 10, the values of .500 and $-.543$ for X_1 and X_9, respectively, indicate that the latter variable has only slightly more weight than the former in explaining the variance in apparel employment growth (Y_{23}) between states. Or, again, of the total amount of stone, clay and glass (Y_{32}) employment growth variation between states that has been statistically explained (41 per cent, $.64^2$), X_1 with a regression coefficient in standard units of .530 accounts for roughly three times that attributable to X_6 (.175).

must pay high wages to attract labor, is quite plausible.) But more than this, the correlation rests, in large measure, on only two observations; Oregon and California, two of the highest-wage states in the country, enjoyed (probably coincidentally) three-fifths of all the growth in lumber manufacturing employment from 1947 to 1954. Accordingly, even apart from its weakness as an analytical construct, the lumber estimating equation, reported in Table 10, is a highly questionable predictive device, resting as it does on just two extreme values. The recommendation here is that lumber be tabled, pending further study—especially study of the natural resource variable.

Furniture and Fixtures (Y_{25})

The furniture industry is almost the identical twin of the apparel industry: the same variables, X_1 and X_9 (population change and wage rates); the same signs, positive and negative, respectively (population growth stimulates and high wages dampen furniture employment growth); the same multiple correlation coefficient, .58 (effecting a parallel jump in explained variance from 15 to 34 per cent); and practically the same relative weight for the two regression coefficients (nearly equal weight). But even given the importance of the roles of population growth and wage rates in the employment growth of both apparel and furniture, roughly two-thirds of the interstate differentials in employment growth of these two industries still remain to be explained. Further explanation may well run largely in terms of the raw material needs of the industries in relation to the natural resource endowments of the various states.

Paper and Allied Products (Y_{26})

Variables X_1, prior population change, and X_{27}, investment in new paper plant and equipment tie for the honor of the highest simple correlation with coefficients of .69. Together they yield a multiple correlation coefficient of .81, raising the level of explained variance from 48 to 66 per cent. This proved to be the best fit attainable among the non-durables, rivalling even those among the generally more readily explainable durables. But, then, it will be recalled that paper manufacturing behaved very much like the durables throughout the analysis in Chapter II. Thus, interstate differentials in paper employment growth (1947–54) are two-thirds explained by interstate differentials in population growth (1939–47) and paper plant investment (1947). A comparison of the regression coefficients in standard units indicates that X_1 and X_{27} have equal weight as explanatory factors.

Coefficients of Correlation of Estimated Average Annual Change in Employment in Major Industry Groups, by States, 1947–1954, with Selected Determinants of State Economic Development

Selected determinants of economic development	Coefficients of Correlation			
	(Y_{24}) Lumber & related products	(Y_{25}) Furniture & fixtures	(Y_{26}) Paper & allied products	(Y_{27}) Printing & publishing
Growth of the local market				
X_1: Average annual change in state population, 1940–47	.32	.39	.69	.66
X_2: Average annual change in state personal income, 1940–47	.16	.36	.66	.46
X_3: Average annual change in state personal income, 1945–48	.10	.20	.50	.26
Industrialization				
X_4: Average annual change in employment in all manufacturing industries, 1939–47	.08	.21	.55	.41
X_5: Expenditures for plant and equipment by all manufacturing industries, 1947	.06	.32	.58	.50
X_6: Average annual number of patents issues to state residents, 1946–48	.18	.18	.50	.32
State and local taxes				
X_7: State and local taxes as a per cent of state personal income, 1953	.15	−.06	−.04	−.22
X_8: Estimated state and local taxes paid by business per non-agricultural employee, 1953	.17	.07	.11	.13
Labor market characteristics				
X_9: Average hourly earnings in manufacturing industries, 1949	.58	−.28	.02	.13
X_{10}: Estimated trade union membership as a per cent of non-agricultural employee, 1947	.45	−.22	.21	.11
Educational levels and facilities				
X_{11}: Median years of school completed by persons twenty-five years old and over, 1950	.54	−.20	−.13	.05

		Coefficients of Correlation			
Selected determinants of economic development		(Y_{24}) Lumber & related products	(Y_{25}) Furniture & fixtures	(Y_{26}) Paper & allied products	(Y_{27}) Printing & publishing
X_{12}:	Number of persons twenty-five years old and over who completed four or more years of college, 1950	.17	.36	.63	.43
X_{13}:	Total staff, institutions of higher education, 1947–48	.10	.35	.58	.34
Industry-specific variables					
X_{14-20}:	Average annual number selected patents issued to state residents, 1947–48				
X_{21-40}:	Expenditures for plant and equipment, by industry, 1947	.57	.33	.69	.36
X_{41-60}:	Employment, by industry, 1947	.07	.32	.51	.10

Table 9c. Coefficients of Correlation of Estimated Average Annual Change in Employment in Major Industry Groups, by States, 1947–1954, with Selected Determinants of State Economic Development

		Coefficients of Correlation			
Selected determinants of economic development		(Y_{28}) Chemicals & allied products	(Y_{29}) Petroleum & coal products	(Y_{30}) Rubber products	(Y_{31}) Leather & leather products
Growth of the local market					
X_1:	Average annual change in state population, 1940–47	.33	.17	− .11	− .08
X_2:	Average annual change in state personal income, 1940–47	.29	.02	.05	− .54
X_3:	Average annual change in state personal income, 1945–48	.22	.01	.07	− .68
Industrialization					
X_4:	Average annual change in employment in all manufacturing industries, 1939–47	.26	.02	− .06	− .65

41

Table 9c (Continued)

Coefficients of Correlation

Selected determinants of economic development	(Y_{28}) Chemicals & allied products	(Y_{29}) Petroleum & coal products	(Y_{30}) Rubber products	(Y_{31}) Leather & leather products
X_5: Expenditures for plant and equipment by all manufacturing industries, 1947	.34	.16	−.10	−.54
X_6: Average annual number of patents issued to state residents, 1946–48	.11	−.09	.07	−.60
State and local taxes				
X_7: State and local taxes as a per cent of state personal income, 1953	−.17	−.23	.04	.25
X_8: Estimated state and local taxes paid by business per non-agricultural employee, 1953	−.15	−.19	−.01	.00
Labor market characteristics				
X_9: Average hourly earnings in manufacturing industries, 1949	−.07	.03	−.08	−.28
X_{10}: Estimated trade union membership as a per cent of non-agricultural employee, 1947	.02	−.03	−.10	−.39
Educational levels and facilities				
X_{11}: Median years of school completed by persons twenty-five years old and over, 1950	−.24	−.12	.01	.10
X_{12}: Number of persons twenty-five years old and over who completed four or more years of college, 1950	.24	−.06	.12	−.52
X_{13}: Total staff, institutions of higher education, 1947–48	.24	−.09	.19	−.60
Industry-specific variables				
$X_{14\text{-}20}$: Average annual number selected patents issued to state residents, 1947–48	.42			
$X_{21\text{-}40}$: Expenditures for plant and equipment, by industry, 1947	.43	.39	−.34	−.50
$X_{41\text{-}60}$: Employment, by industry, 1947	.28	.48	−.42	−.73

Chemicals and Allied Products (Y_{28})

A review of the simple correlation coefficients for chemicals reminds us of the very modest association between employment growth in that industry and any of the sixteen potential growth determinants. The two highest coefficients are for industry-specific variables, investment in chemical plant and equipment (X_{29}) and patent grants connected with chemical products and processes (X_{14}). And these two complement each other so as to produce the highest correlation with the dependent variable (.47) attainable from any combination of independent variables, but only a slight improvement is effected—an increase in explained variance from a level of 18 per cent for either of the two to a level of 22 per cent for a combination of the two. Comparison of the regression coefficients in standard units indicates that these two variables have roughly equal weight. (This is a very mediocre result. A fresh search for additional determinants of employment change in the chemical industry is mandatory; probably the need is for variables more specific to the industry, such as, perhaps, interstate differentials in raw material supplies, and power costs.)

Stone, Clay and Glass Products (Y_{32})

The highest simple correlation in stone, clay and glass was with population growth (X_1), .62, followed by a number of coefficients between .40 and .46. Of these latter, the industry-general patent variable (X_6) made the greatest *net* contribution because it was the least correlated with X_1, that is, its association with the dependent variable duplicated the least that portion of the variation in Y_{32} already explained by X_1. Even so, the addition of X_6 only raises the correlation coefficient from .62 to .64, increasing explained variance from 38 to 41 per cent. One might hazard the guess that the population growth variable applies especially to the stone and clay employment growth, following from the spatially-limited (local) product markets characteristic of these two industry sub-groups; the general patent variable's influence may be largely confined to the glass employment growth, following from the wider markets and more complex technology characteristic of this latter industry and of the industries it serves. At least the results suggest that a breakdown of this major industry group might be revealing. Comparison of the regression coefficients in standard units indicates that X_1 has about three times the weight of X_6.

Table 9d. Coefficients of Correlation of Estimated Average Annual Change in Employment in Major Industry Groups, by States, 1947–1954, with Selected Determinants of State Economic Development

		Coefficients of Correlation			
Selected determinants of economic development		(Y_{32}) Stone, clay & glass products	(Y_{33}) Primary metal industries	(Y_{34}) Fabricated metal products	(Y_{35}) Machinery, except electric
Growth of the local market					
X_1:	Average annual change in state population, 1940–47	.62	.49	.80	.57
X_2:	Average annual change in state personal income, 1940–47	.46	.71	.86	.74
X_3:	Average annual change in state personal income, 1945–48	.33	.67	.74	.71
Industrialization					
X_4:	Average annual change in employment in all manufacturing industries, 1939–47	.42	.70	.76	.74
X_5:	Expenditures for plant and equipment by all manufacturing industries, 1947	.46	.76	.78	.73
X_6:	Average annual number of patents issued to state residents, 1946–48	.44	.58	.76	.69
State and local taxes					
X_7:	State and local taxes as a per cent of state personal income, 1953	−.08	−.25	−.15	−.17
X_8:	Estimated state and local taxes paid by business per non-agricultural employee, 1953	.20	.03	.15	.17
Labor market characteristics					
X_9:	Average hourly earnings in manufacturing industries, 1949	.16	−.27	.32	.38
X_{10}:	Established trade union membership as a per cent of non-agricultural employee, 1947	−.06	.34	.28	.27
Educational levels and facilities					
X_{11}:	Median years of school completed by persons twenty-five years old and over, 1950	.13	.07	.13	.10

44

Table 9d (*Continued*)

Selected determinants of economic development	Coefficients of Correlation			
	(Y_{32}) Stone, clay & glass products	(Y_{33}) Primary metal industries	(Y_{34}) Fabricated metal products	(Y_{35}) Machinery, except electric
X_{12}: Number of persons twenty-five years old and over who completed four or more years of college, 1950	.44	.67	.82	.70
X_{13}: Total staff, institutions of higher education, 1947–48	.35	.68	.74	.65
Industry-specific variables				
X_{14-20}: Average annual number selected patents issued to state residents, 1947–48	.39	.66	.73	.71
X_{21-40}: Expenditures for plant and equipment, by industry, 1947	.37	.78	.72	.59
X_{41-60}: Employment, by industry, 1947	.21	.77	.65	.65

Table 9e. *Coefficients of Correlation of Estimated Average Annual Change in Employment in Major Industry Groups, by States, 1947–1954, with Selected Determinants of State Economic Development*

Selected determinants of economic development	Coefficients of Correlation			
	(Y_{36}) Electrical machinery	(Y_{37}) Transportation equipment	(Y_{38}) Instruments & related products	(Y_{40}) All manufacturing
Growth of the local market				
X_1: Average annual change in state population, 1940–47	.58	.88	.56	.90
X_2: Average annual change in state personal income, 1940–47	.82	.74	.79	.86
X_3: Average annual change in state personal income, 1945–48	.76	.53	.73	.68
Industrialization				
X_4: Average annual change in employment in all manufacturing industries, 1939–47	.78	.59	.76	.73

Table 9e (Continued)

Selected determinants of economic development	Coefficients of Correlation			
	(Y_{36}) Electrical machinery	(Y_{37}) Transpor- tation equipment	(Y_{38}) Instruments & related products	(Y_{40}) All manu- facturing
X_5: Expenditures for plant and equipment by all manufac- turing industries, 1947	.78	.62	.79	.76
X_6: Average annual number of patents issued to state resi- dents, 1946–48	.84	.58	.82	.70
State and local taxes				
X_7: State and local taxes as a per cent of state personal in- come, 1953	$-.19$	$-.17$	$-.22$	$-.19$
X_8: Estimated state and local taxes paid by business per non-agricultural employee, 1953	.28	.16	.27	.18
Labor market characteristics				
X_9: Average hourly earnings in manufacturing industries, 1949	.33	.36	.30	.33
X_{10}: Estimated trade union mem- bership as a per cent of non- agricultural employee, 1947	.34	.25	.32	.28
Educational levels and facilities				
X_{11}: Median years of school com- pleted by persons twenty- five years old and over, 1950	.14	.24	.08	.13
X_{12}: Number of persons twenty- five years old and over who completed four or more years of college, 1950	.84	.71	.78	.84
X_{13}: Total staff, institutions of higher education, 1947–48	.82	.63	.72	.76
Industry-specific variables				
X_{14-20}: Average annual number se- lected patents issued to state residents, 1947–48		.54	.69	
X_{21-40}: Expenditures for plant and equipment, by industry, 1947	.22	.33	.51	.76
X_{41-60}: Employment, by industry, 1947	.80	.48	.59	.65

Primary Metal Industries (Y_{33})

The primary metal industries group displays a pattern of correlation coefficients which is typical of the durable goods industries in general—high correlation with all but the two tax variables $(X_{7,\,8})$, the two labor force variables $(X_{9,\,10})$ and the mass education variable (X_{11}). Beginning with a simple correlation coefficient of .78 for expenditures on new primary metal plant and equipment (X_{34}), the addition of the number of college educated state residents (X_{12}) boosts the correlation coefficient to .82, for an increase in explained variance from 61 to 67 per cent. But basic-metal plant investment and the college educated labor supply could be replaced with various (but not all) combinations of the following: industry employment in the origin year (the locational inertia variable, X_{54}), all manufacturing investment (X_5), prior change in personal income (X_2), prior change in manufacturing employment (the accelerator variant, X_4), the supply of college staff (X_{13}) and general and selective patent indexes (X_6 and X_{16}) with nearly as good results. Close decisions between alternative forms of the estimating equation are characteristic of all of the durable goods industries due to the high inter-correlation between the many measures of industrial maturity we have collected. For the estimating equation chosen, $Y_{33} = f(X_{12,\,34})$, a comparison of the regression coefficients in standard units indicates that X_{34} has about 1.8 times the weight of X_{12}.

Fabricated Metal Products (Y_{34})

The simple correlation coefficients for fabricated metals run much higher than for any of the preceding industries—only three of the independent variables fall short of statistical significance, the two tax indexes $(X_{7,\,8})$ and the mass education index (X_{11}). From this rich selection, a combination of population growth (X_1) and personal income growth (X_2) give the best mix, despite the high correlation between the two (.71). The simple correlation of .86 for X_2 with Y_{34} is raised to .90 when X_1 is added, boosting the explained variance from 74 to 81 per cent. The signs of both variables are, of course, positive; the equation expresses a two-faceted, growth-of-the-local-market effect. A comparison of the regression coefficients in standard units indicates that X_2 has approximately 1.6 times the weight of X_1. (Patent grants associated with fabricated metal products, X_{17}, combine with personal income growth to produce a second best equation.)

Machinery, Except Electrical (Y_{35})

In the analysis of employment growth in machinery manufacturing, the preceding growth of all manufacturing (X_4) and population (X_1) combine to produce a multiple correlation of .78. This combination of variables raises the level of explained variance from 55 per cent (X_4 alone) to 61 per cent (X_4 and X_1). (An alternative equation with X_{18}, machinery-industry-associated patent grants, substituted for the population-growth variable, X_1, produced a second best formulation.) The signs of both variables (positive) agree with *a priori* expectations; the equation expresses the influence of the growth of the local market in two forms: increasing household demand via a growing population and increasing industrial demand via an increasing amount of manufacturing activity—a growing business population. A comparison of the regression coefficients in standard units indicates that X_4 has approximately 1.7 times the weight of X_1.

Electrical Machinery (Y_{36})

Electrical machinery appears, at first impression, to introduce the delightful dilemma of an embarrassment of riches, with five simple correlation coefficients of .80 or over and another three between .75 and .80. From this field of strong candidates, the general, all-patent index (X_6) and prior population change (X_1) conjoin to yield a multiple correlation coefficient of .86. But this is only a very modest improvement over the .84 correlation of X_6 alone, and explained variance rises only slightly from 71 to 74 per cent. Clearly, many alternative formulations would give almost as good results; the supply of college graduates (X_{12}), for example, matches the 71 per cent explained variance of X_6. The lack of any appreciable gain through effecting various combinations of variables is ascribable, of course, to the high intercorrelation between these various independent variables. A comparison of the regression coefficients in standard units indicates that X_6 has 3.5 times the weight of X_1 as an explanatory factor.

Transportation Equipment (Y_{37})

It proved to be very difficult to improve significantly on the simple correlation between population growth (X_1) and employment growth in the transportation equipment industry, a coefficient of .88. Alternative formulations, one with the addition of X_4 (prior growth in manufacturing activity) and another with the addition of X_{19} (internal-combustion-engine patent grants) could only lift the correlation coefficient to .89 and the explained variance from 77 to 79 per cent. Comparison of the regression coefficients in standard units indicates that X_1 has approximately four times the weight of X_4 and five times the weight of X_{19}.

But an inspection of Figure 18 in Appendix E suggests that the formulation of an equation with which to estimate employment change in the transportation equipment industry awaits a basic reformulation of the model. (For an explanation of the origin and derivation of this figure see Chapter V.) The location trend (1947–54) of transportation equipment was decidedly one of decentralization *and regionalization*. This industry shifted its relative weight away from Michigan (and the other northern industrial states from New Jersey to Wisconsin, except Ohio) to a limited number of widely-dispersed states. Roughly, the pattern changed from a single nucleus to a multiple-nuclei form, without any notable tendency toward diffusion. Rapidly growing pockets formed at near regularly spaced intervals; emerging centers in Washington, California-Arizona, Kansas-Missouri, Texas, New York-Connecticut and Georgia present a clean, almost classic, picture of regionalization.

What all of this suggests is that, if our correlation analysis were reformulated on a larger-than-state regional basis, an estimating equation with a much closer fit could be constructed. Or, more simply said, we might be able to make a reasonably good estimate of the employment trend for southeastern United States, but whether the predicted change takes place in Alabama, Georgia or South Carolina seems to be beyond the capacity of our present formula. Perhaps the strongest moral to be drawn from this experience is that the spatial positions of the various states should not be ignored—some map-making is in order. This is not, however, a clarion call for a lot of indiscriminate coloring of outline maps of the United States. (Some farther observations on the role of spatial measurement are appended to Chapter V.)

Instruments and Related Products (Y_{38})

Employment growth in instruments is most closely correlated (.82) with the general, all-patents index (X_6). The best that can be achieved through multiple correlation is an almost negligible increase in the correlation coefficient to .83, through the addition of the all manufacturing investment index (X_5). Alternatively, a substantial portion of the interstate variation in instrument employment growth can be statistically explained, in turn, by corresponding interstate variations in prior personal income change (X_2) or the supply of college graduates (X_{12}) or prior change in all manufacturing employment (X_4). But no combination of them makes any appreciable improvement in the statistical fit, reflecting again the high inter-correlation between this set of independent variables. The fact that instrument industry employment is more closely correlated to the all-patent index than it is to the instrument-industry-associated patent index probably signifies that either the broader, former index is even more representative of instrument technology than the narrower, custom made, latter index, a distinct possibility, or the industry is more locationally attracted to the generally technologically progressive areas (the markets for tools) than to the sources of supply of new instruments (the residences of instrument inventors). A comparison of the regression coefficients in standard units indicates that X_6 has 1.5 times the weight of X_5 as an explanatory factor.

All Manufacturing (Y_{40})

Considering the frequency with which prior population change (X_1) has appeared as a leading variable in the analysis of the various sub-groups of manufacturing, it would indeed be surprising if this odds-on favorite did not win a place in the all manufacturing estimating equation. Following the population variable (.90) is the closely related market-growth factor, prior change in personal income (X_2), with a coefficient of .86, followed in turn by the supply of college graduates (X_{12}) at .84. In the best statistical fit, X_1 and X_2 unite to raise the correlation markedly to .95, accordantly raising the explained variance from 81 per cent for X_1 alone to an un-paralled 90 per cent for the two variables combined. To restate this result, interstate differentials in annual average, over-the-war, population growth (1940–47) and personal income growth (1940–47) explain 90 per cent of the variation between the states in the absolute growth of all manufacturing employment in the postwar period (1947–54). This suggests the dominant importance of the market as an industrial location factor for manufacturing in general, as well as for a majority of the sub-groups (X_1 appears in eight out of twelve of the industry estimating equations). A comparison of the regression coefficients in standard units indicates that X_1 has 1.3 times the weight of X_2 as an explanatory factor. All thirteen estimating equations are set forth in Table 10.

In Summary

The central role, throughout, of the growth of the local market is the single most outstanding feature of the multi-variate analysis. Population growth in the preceding period (X_1) plays a leading role in eight out of twelve of the manufacturing sub-groups, with the companion variable, prior personal income change (X_2), complementing it in one industry (fabricated metals) and standing by in the wings as the second best alterna-tive in most of the remaining cases. And these two facets of local demand pull near equal weight in the aggregative all manufacturing estimating equation.

Expenditures on plant and equipment in the related industry ($X_{21\text{-}40}$)

Apparel & related products:
$$Y_{23} = 2{,}526.3 + \overset{(.500)}{\underset{(1.18)}{4.83\ X_1}} - \overset{(-.543)}{\underset{(404)}{1{,}798\ X_9}} \pm 529 \qquad R = .58$$

Lumber & products:
$$Y_{24} = -2{,}637.4 + \overset{(.462)}{\underset{(413)}{1{,}807\ X_9}} + \overset{(.448)}{\underset{(1.41)}{6.00\ X_{25}}} \pm 548 \quad R = .72$$

Furniture & fixtures:
$$Y_{25} = 856.2 + \overset{(.530)}{\underset{(0.51)}{2.15\ X_1}} - \overset{(-.445)}{\underset{(176)}{618\ X_9}} \pm 230 \qquad R = .58$$

Paper & allied products:
$$Y_{26} = 57.4 + \overset{(.468)}{\underset{(1.40)}{2.13\ X_1}} + \overset{(.479)}{\underset{(0.96)}{1.49\ X_{27}}} \pm 186 \qquad R = .81$$

Chemicals & allied products:
$$Y_{28} = 251.5 + \overset{(.250)}{\underset{(1.39)}{2.12\ X_{14}}} + \overset{(.273)}{\underset{(3.98)}{6.62\ X_{29}}} \pm 593 \qquad R = .47$$

Stone, clay & glass products:
$$Y_{32} = -39.4 + \overset{(.530)}{\underset{(0.58)}{2.35\ X_1}} + \overset{(.175)}{\underset{(0.476)}{0.686\ X_6}} \pm 238 \qquad R = .64$$

Primary metal industries:
$$Y_{33} = 124.1 + \overset{(.320)}{\underset{(0.62)}{1.88\ X_{12}}} + \overset{(.586)}{\underset{(3.54)}{19.68\ X_{34}}} \pm 463 \qquad R = .82$$

Fabricated metal products:
$$Y_{34} = -116.9 + \overset{(.370)}{\underset{(1.03)}{4.21\ X_1}} + \overset{(.601)}{\underset{(1.8)}{12.2\ X_2}} \pm 343 \qquad R = .90$$

Machinery, except electrical:
$$Y_{35} = 45.7 + \overset{(.257)}{\underset{(2.0)}{11.2\ X_1}} + \overset{(.613)}{\underset{(7.8)}{18.4\ X_4}} \pm 800 \qquad R = .78$$

Electrical machinery:
$$Y_{36} = -53.6 + \overset{(.212)}{\underset{(7.41)}{5.69\ X_1}} + \overset{(.735)}{\underset{(6.05)}{16.07\ X_6}} \pm 925 \qquad R = .86$$

Transportation equipment:
$$Y_{37} = -319.7 + \overset{(.782)}{\underset{(5.5)}{56.0\ X_1}} + \overset{(.188)}{\underset{(21.6)}{52.8\ X_4}} \pm 2{,}233 \quad R = .89$$

Instruments & related products:
$$Y_{38} = -30.3 + \overset{(.347)}{\underset{(0.34)}{0.74\ X_5}} + \overset{(.520)}{\underset{(0.63)}{2.06\ X_6}} \pm 185 \qquad R = .83$$

All manufacturing:
$$Y_{40} = 3{,}521.7 + \overset{(.573)}{\underset{(3.28)}{92.92\ X_1}} + \overset{(.456)}{\underset{(5.8)}{131.9\ X_2}} \pm 3{,}436 \quad R = .95$$

where:

Y: Estimated average annual change in total employment in the state, 1947–54;

X_1: Average annual change in state population, 1940–47 (in thousands);

X_2: Average annual change in state personal income, 1940–47 (in tens of millions of dollars);

Table 10 (Continued)

X_4:   Average annual change in manufacturing employment in the state, 1939–47 (in thousands);

X_5:   Expenditures for new plant and equipment in all manufacturing industries, 1947 (in millions of dollars);

X_6:   Average annual number of patents issued to state residents, 1946–48 (in tens);

X_9:   Average hourly earnings in manufacturing industries in the state, 1949 (in dollars);

X_{12}:   Number of persons twenty-five years and over with four or more years of college, 1950 (in thousands);

X_{14}:   Number of patents granted to state residents in patent classes: 18, 23, 71, 204, 260, in 1947

X_{25}:   Expenditures for new plant and equipment in lumber manufacturing, 1947, (in hundreds of dollars);

X_{27}:   Expenditures for new plant and equipment in paper manufacturing, 1947, (in hundreds of thousand of dollars);

X_{29}:   Expenditures for new plant and equipment in chemicals manufactured, 1947 (in millions of dollars);

X_{34}:   Expenditures for new plant and equipment in primary metal manufacturing, 1947 (in millions of dollars);

* *The figure in the parentheses below the regression coefficient is the standard error of the coefficient in original units and the figure above is the regression coefficient in standard units.*

enter into the best estimating equation in four of the twelve industry groups: lumber, paper, chemicals and steel. (Interestingly, each of the four industries has a strong natural resource orientation.) More attention to the industry-specific *type* of variable deserves a high priority in any further studies, especially with respect to the natural-resource-oriented non-durables, wherein estimating performance has been the poorest to date.

The general patent index (X_6) contributed to the best statistical fit in three industries: stone, clay and glass; electrical machinery; and instruments. Complementarily, the selective patent index (X_{14}) made the chemical industry equation. In addition, these other selective patent indexes, X_{17}, X_{18} and X_{19}, make nearly as good a showing as did the second variable in the equations for fabricated metal products, non-electrical machinery and transportation equipment, respectively. In view of the possibilities for further refinement here, the more-than-modest success experienced with patents, our most unconventional variable, is one of the more heartening results of the study.

Prior change in manufacturing employment, the variant on the accelerator (X_4), entered the best estimating equation twice: non-electrical machinery and transportation equipment. The machinery industry is, significantly, that industry for which the *a priori* case for the existence of a force of locational pull through derived demand is one of the strongest, perhaps the strongest. And this same variable holds considerable promise in metals, electrical machinery and instruments—the other capital goods industries.

Average hourly earnings (X_9) appears to be a major determinant of employment growth in the apparel and furniture industries, with growth spurred by low wage rates and dampened by high wage rates.

One of the most surprising developments is the absence of the origin-year-employment variable (X_{41-60}) from the list of factors which enter the best estimating equations. In no case was the beginning amount of employment in the industry either the first or second leading determinant of the amount of employment growth sustained subsequently. Size has not dominated the amount of change experienced. (Although the origin-year-employment variable was the next best alternative to those selected in a number of cases.)

The tax and unionization variables did not enter any of the final employment estimating equations and only one representation of the educational variables was recorded. The fact that these variables, with a single exception, did not make the "first team" should not be construed to imply that they are of little or no significance in state industrial development; only the early returns have come in. Subsequent refinements in both data and analytical technique will almost certainly shift emphases and rearrange linkages within the model.

IV

AN EXTENSION OF THE ANALYSIS TO THE RATE OF GROWTH OF MANUFACTURING EMPLOYMENT

At the outset, we decided to measure growth in absolute rather than in relative terms. The dependent variable became average annual change in employment, although we rejected a related expression of growth, *rate* of change in employment, neither summarily nor without considerable misgivings. This hard choice was forced by considerations of time and budget. Fortunately, circumstances changed sufficiently to allow the analyses of absolute change to be complemented by parallel analyses couched in rates of change, although these latter have had to be treated more briefly.

Problems of Measurement

Small Bases and Lack of Data

The major difficulty encountered in formulating a rate-of-growth variant of our model was, as anticipated in Chapter I, the treatment of the inordinately high rates of change that can and frequently do emanate from very small bases. The Mountain states, in particular, often registered annual rates of change in excess of 20 per cent, compounded, magnitudes which often could have resulted from the chance location of even a single new plant. Therefore, despite the extra work and the risk of challenge involved, we subjected the data to a substantial amount of editing to eliminate extreme values that could easily have been due to pure chance. While we followed, usually, no simple, mechanical formula for eliminating data, any state growth-rate that substantially exceeded that of the next highest state was discarded if the base employment from which it was measured was less than one thousand workers. For example, the annual growth rate of 18.36 per cent for stone, clay and glass employment in Nevada is substantially in excess of the next highest rate, 9.80 per cent (Rhode Island), and is almost beyond comparison with the national average rate of 1.65 per cent. Since Nevada's rapid growth rate rests on the slender 1947 employment base of only 407 stone, clay and glass workers, the state was eliminated from the sample. An *unabridged* set of the annual employ-ment growth-rates, state by state, industry by industry, is presented in Appendix A, Table A-2, together with a list of the data deleted. The reader is offered the opportunity to assure himself as to the neutrality of the data editing—or just to idly second guess, if so inclined.

A second problem posed by the dependent variable in its newly-altered form is the proper treatment of states for which no data was reported. Previously, in the absence of data for a given manufacturing activity in a given state (e.g., for instruments in Oregon or for fourteen out of the twenty manufacturing classifications in North Dakota), the average annual change in employment was estimated to be zero. The rationale offered for this practice is that no data usually signifies that the industry in question is of very small size in that state and such employment change as did occur was probably of very small magnitude, rendering zero a reason-ably good approximation in most cases. But no parallel procedure is possible here; the imputation of a growth rate of 0 per cent (no change) is not warranted; in fact, what is most likely is that, starting from such a small base, the actual growth rate is very much above that level. The best practice seemed to be to eliminate those states.[11] Thus, through elimina-tions, due both to inordinately high growth rates and to the absence of data, the number of observations (states compared) varies from forty-two for twelve major industry groups to a low of fourteen for tobacco manu-factures. (For further discussion of the mechanics of setting up the set of dependent variables see the note to Table A-2 of Appendix A.)

Alterations in the Independent Variables

The shift from absolute change to rate of change as the dependent variable of the model necessitated a parallel modification in many of the

[11] In fact, Professor John B. Lansing of the University of Michigan argues that it might have been better to have deleted the zeros in the dependent variable from the correlations of Chapter II, the absolute growth formulation. He suggests that states could be divided into two groups, those in which the industry is represented and those in which it is not, and the analysis of growth could then be focused on only those areas wherein the industry is located. Certainly, a good case can be made for eliminating the have-not states, especially when they are also can-not-be states, as in the case of industries locationally tied to some scarce (locationally spotty) natural resource. Still, probably at least as often, the zeros may represent the continuing absence of a given industry in places where it could and would develop, except for the adverse local conditions expressed by the independent variable(s) with which the industrial growth series is correlated. And, of course, if our set of independent variables ever became sufficiently inclusive, all zeros would be explained by the proper multiple regression equation. Even so, Professor Lansing's suggestion that sub-sets of the states be analyzed demands serious consideration in any future re-formulations of the model. Unfortunately, neither time nor budget would permit a re-run of the data along the lines of his suggestion.

associated independent variables. For consistency, absolute changes had to be transformed into rates of change, absolute numbers had to be re-expressed as ratios, while existing ratios could remain unchanged. The altered forms of the various independent variables are as follows:

Independent Variables in the Rate-of-Growth Model

X_1': Annual rate of change in state population, 1940–47.

X_2': Annual rate of change in state personal income, 1940–47.

X_3': Annual rate of change in state personal income, 1945–48.

X_4': Annual rate of change in total manufacturing employment, by states, 1939–47.

X_5': Expenditures for new plant and equipment in all manufacturing industries per manufacturing employee, by states, 1947.

X_6': Average annual number of patents and designs issued to residents per 100,000 residents, by states, 1946–48.

X_7: State and local taxes as a per cent of state personal income, by states, 1953.

X_8: Estimated state and local taxes paid by non-agricultural business per employee, by states, 1953.

X_9: Average hourly earnings in manufacturing industries, by states, 1949.

X_{10}: Estimated trade union membership as a per cent of non-agricultural employment by states, 1947.

X_{11}: Median years of school completed by persons twenty-five years old and over, by states, 1950.

X_{12}': Per cent of persons twenty-five years old and over who have completed four or more years of college, by states, 1950.

X_{13}': Total staff at institutions of higher education (1947–48) as a per cent of persons twenty-five years old and over (1950), by states.[12]

X_{41-60}': Industry employment (1947) as a per cent of total employment (1950), by states.[13]

Nature of the Alteration of the Independent Variables

X_1: From absolute change to rate of change

X_2: From absolute change to rate of change

X_3: From absolute change to rate of change

X_4: From absolute change to rate of change

[12] The denominator of the ratio applies to the year 1950 because data on the adult population, by states, appears not to be available for any year nearer to 1947-48 than 1950.

[13] The denominator of the ratio applies to the year 1950 because data on total employment, by states, appears not to be available for any year nearer to 1947 than 1950; the industry employment figures for 1950 were much less complete than for 1947 (a manufacturing census year), so a balanced 1950 ratio could not be constructed.

X_5:   From an absolute number to a ratio
X_6:   From an absolute number to a ratio
X_7:   No change, remains a ratio
X_8:   No change, remains a ratio
X_9:   No change, remains a ratio
X_{10}:   No change, remains a ratio
X_{11}:   No change, remains a ratio
X_{12}:   From an absolute number to a ratio
X_{13}:   From an absolute number to a ratio
$X_{41\text{-}60}$:   From an absolute number to a ratio

Bigness and Bias

With the hypotheses and accompanying rationale underlying the selection of the various independent variables remaining intact, it is unnecessary to weave again the basic fabric of the model, after the fashion of Chapter I. Again, the functional relationships are the same as before (linear), although the form of the variables is now changed. But before attempting to digest this new batch of correlations, it would be well to develop, at some length, the distinctly different character of the two dependent variables.

The original version of the model harbors an implicit bias toward positive correlation. This was especially true when change was correlated with change, $X_{1\text{-}4}$. Ordinarily, those states which add the greater amount of population (X_1), personal income $(X_{2, 3})$ and/or manufacturing employment (X_4) can be expected to add the greater number of workers in the various manufacturing industries. This is not to say that pure or even near tautologies have been allowed to adulterate the model; it was *prior* population change (1940–47) which was correlated with *subsequent* employment growth (1947–54) and so forth. Still, large size (e.g., the northern states) is especially compatible with large change on both sides of the correlation; a size-with-size bias is evident, producing a bias toward direct association or positive correlation. Further, the variables which are expressed in absolute numbers $(X_{5, 6, 12, 13})$ are also subject to this effect. Those states which enjoy the greater dollar amount of manufacturing investment (X_5), number of patents (X_6), number of college graduates (X_{12}) and number of college faculty (X_{13}) should probably experience the greater addition of new workers, more often than not. (Conversely, variables $X_{7\text{-}11}$ are ex- expressed, in one form or another, as ratios—are deflated—and are, therefore not subject to this positive correlation bias.)

As against this size-with-size bias in some of the absolute-growth correlations, no bias toward positive coefficients characterizes the rate-of-growth variant—size has been deflated into rates and ratios throughout. Quite the reverse, the bias in this latter model is toward negative correlation. Investment, patents, taxes, wage rates, unionization and education are all facets of, as well as factors in, industrial development and, therefore, the more industrially advanced states would normally rank high in these measures, even when deflated into ratios. But, at the same time, these industrially advanced states tend to be constrained in growth-rate by the very fact of their high level of industrial development; it is exceedingly difficult for one of the big industrial states to grow at a rapid *rate*, especially in its speciality. (If, starting in 1947, the Michigan transportation equipment industry had grown at the 1947–54 Georgia rate, Michigan would have absorbed the entire national employment in that industry by 1951. Michigan was pushing against the ceiling.) Thus, the linking of development-ratios which tend to be directly associated with industrial maturity and growth-rates which tend to be inversely associated with industrial maturity creates an implicit bias toward negative correlation between the ratios and growth-rates. Positive correlations are, therefore, as hard to come by for some of the variables in the rate-of-growth model as they were commonplace in the earlier, absolute growth version. And low, negative correlations should be treated as circumspectly in the analyses to follow as low, positive correlations were above.

Correlation Results: Bi-variate Analysis

The Degree of Local Specialization in the Industry

Suppose, then, that a critical factor in industrial growth-rates is how far the growth has already progressed. Now, if a common, conventional logistic growth curve characterized the manufacturing employment growth pattern in each of the states, the forecaster would need but to locate that state's present position along the curve to foretell the coming rate of change. But states are, of course, climbing up and sliding down *individual* (and perhaps even unique) growth curves, which curves are probably altering their shapes continually. Lacking the ability to define the many growth curves, what even approximate measure of the state of development of a given industry in a given state can we come by? An absolute measure, such as the number of workers locally employed in the industry, must be rejected for the obvious reason that the various states have vastly different industrial potentials—ceilings within which their growth is constrained. To illustrate, New York starting with 138,000 non-electrical machinery workers in 1947 still had plenty of room in which to grow and did grow, 1947–54, and at a much faster annual rate (2.75 per cent) than the national average rate (1.86 per cent); that much local employment in 1947 would have nearly exhausted Rhode Island's employment potential in *all* manufacturing industries, at least through to 1954. But physical size is not the primary test; most of the spacious Western states, remote from the big markets, will probably reach a state of surfeit in most manufacturing industries well short of the absolute employment that has already been attained in most of the moderate- to small-sized East North Central and Middle Atlantic states.

Alternatively, the current level of local employment in a given industry might be related to the total employment in that area. The presumption here would be that a community has less room to grow in those industries in which it has specialized than it has in those in which it has lagged; the larger the current role of a given manufacturing industry in a given state, the smaller the subsequent rate of growth of that industry in that state. This line of reasoning, clearly, runs afoul of all the forces which tend to produce and perpetuate regional specialization—that is, situations wherein "them that have gets." But the purpose here is not to establish the existence of any universal tendency toward conformity (balance) in state industrial structures; the question is: Are rates of growth in manufacturing employment negatively correlated with the existing degree of specialization in that industry and are the observed relationships such as to be useful in a predictive context? Toward this end, employment in each of the major industry groups was expressed as a per cent of total state employment (non-manufacturing as well as manufacturing) and correlated with the respective employment growth-rates of these industries ($X'_{41\text{-}60}$ $Y'_{20\text{-}40}$). In effect, this set of correlations expresses a functional relationship which roughly parallels the implicit bias against bigness argued above and, indeed, can be used to test the actual existence of the presumed anti-bigness bias in rate-of-growth formulations.

The high promise of using the current degree of specialization in an industry as an aid in predicting the coming rate of growth of that industry is attested to by the favorable correlation results. The degree of specialization variable exhibited an overall level of simple correlation coefficients which rivalled the very best performances among the thirteen general-form variables. Two-thirds of the industries displayed at least an appreciable level of negative correlation and well over half of these associations were statistically significant. The high point was reached for all manufacturing, with 44 per cent of the interstate differentials in employment growth-rates explained by the state's proportion of total employment in manufacturing in the origin year; the states most highly specialized in manufacturing tended to grow at the slowest rates, confirming the hypothesized anti-bigness bias argued above. And this inverse relationship between degree of specialization and rate of growth carries through many of the sub-classes, entering the best multi-variate estimating equations in apparel, furniture, printing, petroleum, and fabricated metals and just missing out in many of the other industry groups. The full set of simple correlation coefficients for the rate-of-growth variant of the model are presented in Table 11.

Rate-of-Growth with Rate-of-Growth Correlations

The bias against bigness in the dependent variable of the rate-of-growth model leads to bias toward negative correlation only when it is not offset by a similar bias against bigness in the associated independent variable. A bias against bigness, however, characterizes variables on both sides of the correlation in the case of the first four growth factors (X'_{1-4}). The tendency for the big industrial states to have relative low rates of growth in manufacturing employment is matched by the tendency of these same states to have experienced low rates of growth in population (X'_1), personal income $(X'_{2, 3})$ and manufacturing employment (X'_4) in the preceding time period. Therefore, if anything, the bias in the X'_{1-4} Y'_{20-40} correlations would be toward positive coefficients. Such a bias does exist but, evidently, either this bias is not nearly so strong as the pro-bigness bias which characterizes these same variables in their absolute form or the functional relationships here involved are not nearly so well expressed in geometric form (as rates of change) as they were previously expressed in arithmetic form (as absolute amounts of change). This follows from a comparison of the relevant simple correlation coefficients; the population and personal-income growth coefficients are substantially lower now.

In the original model, the growth of the local market (X_{1-3}) and the locational accelerator (X_4) were among the variables most closely associated with subsequent growth in manufacturing employment, with prior population change (X_1) dominating the employment estimating equations. Now, in this latter model, of the twenty industry groups, only all manufacturing employment growth is at all closely associated with the rate of prior population growth (X'_1). True, the over-the-war rate of personal income change (X'_2) exhibits significant positive correlations with subsequent employment growth rates in textiles, apparel, paper, chemicals, fabricated metals, machinery and instruments, and all manufacturing but at a much lower level than earlier. (Typically, personal income change, 1940–47, explains less than two-fifths of the interstate variation in all manufacturing employment growth, 1947–54, in rate of growth terms as

Table 11. Coefficients of Correlation of Selected Measures of Regional Economic Development with Estimated Annual Rate of Change in Employment, 1947–1954, by States, by Major Manufacturing Industry Group

Major industry group	Market growth			Industrialization			Taxes		Labor		Educational			Spe-cialization
	X'_1	X'_2	X'_3	X'_4	X'_5	X'_6	X_7	X_8	X_9	X_{10}	X_{11}	X_{12}	X'_{13}	X'_{41-60}
Y'_{20}: Food & kindred products	.15	.11	−.24	−.18	.06	−.09	.03	−.14	−.52	−.50	−.27	−.15	−.33	−.28
Y'_{21}: Tobacco manufactures	−.06	.30	−.17	−.31	.54	−.51	.12	−.40	−.49	−.15	−.31	−.40	−.35	.36
Y'_{22}: Textile-mill products	.23	.48	−.35	.16	.24	−.18	−.16	−.44	−.23	−.21	−.23	−.11	−.35	.04
Y'_{23}: Apparel & related products	.05	.38	−.51	−.06	.06	−.17	.10	−.22	−.42	−.32	−.22	−.14	−.35	.21
Y'_{24}: Lumber & related products	.15	.01	.29	.25	−.05	.06	.24	.27	.55	.39	.45	.32	.24	.00
Y'_{25}: Furniture & fixtures	.07	.14	−.28	−.22	.09	−.16	.04	−.02	−.49	−.35	−.25	−.13	−.34	−.20
Y'_{26}: Paper & allied products	.17	.54	−.16	.22	.30	−.36	.16	−.20	−.20	−.14	−.16	−.22	−.33	−.31
Y'_{27}: Printing & publishing	.23	.29	−.21	.06	.17	.01	.02	−.07	−.43	−.59	−.24	.07	−.22	−.54
Y'_{28}: Chemicals & allied products	.26	.52	−.12	.23	.31	−.28	.18	−.11	.06	.09	.07	.12	−.12	−.24
Y'_{29}: Petroleum & coal products	−.04	.28	.22	.10	.27	−.38	−.02	−.20	.03	.01	−.01	−.15	−.06	−.55
Y'_{30}: Rubber products	−.21	−.19	.43	.04	.00	−.14	.15	−.26	−.04	−.58	.11	.21	.46	−.17
Y'_{31}: Leather & leather products	.07	.20	−.31	.03	.12	−.10	.22	.16	.29	.31	.20	.13	.01	−.08
Y'_{32}: Stone, clay & glass products	.13	.59	−.35	−.21	.06	.27	.10	.13	−.34	−.49	.09	.17	.08	−.38
Y'_{33}: Primary metal industries	.30	.13	.10	.21	.45	.06	−.01	−.05	.32	.18	.28	.30	−.01	.02
Y'_{34}: Fabricated metal products	.19	.60	−.32	.12	.20	−.50	.38	−.08	−.28	−.27	.12	.00	−.11	−.52
Y'_{35}: Machinery, except electrical	.14	.43	−.25	.07	.25	−.30	.29	−.04	−.15	−.28	−.07	.11	.17	−.38
Y'_{36}: Electrical machinery	.32	.24	−.25	.23	.41	−.34	.12	−.09	−.17	−.42	.14	.13	.03	−.37
Y'_{37}: Transportation equipment	−.09	.06	−.17	.13	.06	.09	−.01	.00	−.04	−.18	.02	.15	−.02	−.10
Y'_{38}: Instruments & related products	.28	.45	.19	.39	.55	.22	.33	.15	−.01	.34	.27	.14	.05	−.41
Y'_{40}: All manufacturing	.37	.62	−.13	.53	.49	−.25	.27	−.13	.06	−.19	.24	.31	.01	−.66

against nearly twice that level of explained variance when the correlation was couched in absolute terms.) Further, only rubber products manufacturing is significantly associated, directly, with the rate of personal income change for the shorter, postwar period (X_3'); the host of negative correlations registered are probably neither causally significant nor useful in forecasting. And, finally, the rate-of-growth version of the locational accelerator (prior rate of growth of manufacturing employment, X_4') exhibits a singularly unimpressive set of simple correlation coefficients, except for all manufacturing (.53, for a 28 per cent association) and instruments (.39, for a 15 per cent association.) Admittedly, though, these two industry groups are ones in which an acceleration linkage is especially logical.

Considering the foregoing remarks, it is rather surprising to find variables X_1' and X_2' appearing in roughly two-thirds of the rate-of-growth employment estimating equations developed below. The explanation of this seeming paradox is that the growth of the local market, while not nearly as dominant as before, is still significantly associated with manufacturing employment growth rates, especially if various complementary and offsetting factors are taken into consideration, as in multiple correlation and regression analysis.

Investment and Patents

All manufacturing new plant and equipment expenditures per employee (X_5') and all patents per 100,000 population (X_6') are independent variables in ratio form and are, therefore, presumably biased toward inverse association with the dependent variable. If such a bias does exist in the investment-per-employee correlations, however, it is clearly recessive; no statistically significant negative correlations appear, while a rash of positive correlations materialize, descending from a high in instruments of .55 for a 30 per cent association down to lesser associations in tobacco (29 per cent), all manufacturing (24 per cent), primary metals (20) and electrical machinery (16). Even so, these correlations are considerably lower than their counterparts in the absolute-growth model. In contrast, the all-patents variable, which ran along on even terms with the all manufacturing-investment variable in absolute growth, appears to have little value as an explanatory factor in the matter of growth rates. With only a few very weak positive correlations and the dominant, negative coefficients probably of little theoretical or practical consequence, this variable failed to appear in any of the rate-of-growth employment estimating equations which follow.

The gist of these results would seem to be that current patent-intensity is a much better measure of the level of industrial maturity of an area than is current investment intensity and, to repeat, since the more industrially mature areas tend to grow at relatively slow rates, if at all, the bias toward negative correlation probably (more than) washes out whatever linkage there is between patents and growth rates, while this is less true of investment. Either that, or investment is so much stronger than patents as a growth stimulus that the former but not the latter overrides the restraining effect that a high *level* of industrialization has on the generation of further industrialization at a high *rate* of change.

State and Local Taxes

Of the many considerations that culminated in the decision to extend this study to growth rates, none was stronger than the results of the investigation of the influence of taxes on employment growth. To conclude, as above, that "no significant evidence was uncovered to connect state and local tax levels with *interstate* differentials in employment growth in *broad* industry classes" is to tilt the scales on a public policy matter of considerable weight. While our conclusions were delimited and guarded, to even enter this controversy would seem to involve a moral obligation to pursue the question as far as data, techniques and time permit.

Such uneasiness as was felt in dismissing the tax factor stemmed mainly from the nature of the dependent variable—the index of growth. In fact, it was at this point in the study that the possibility of a bias toward bigness made its first compelling impression. Clearly, the big industrial states of the north enjoy such a headstart on the other states that it is virtually impossible for the latter to gain a greater *absolute number* of employees during a short (seven-year) time period and, since the northern states are, in general, high-tax states, a negative correlation is hard to come by—especially in the northern dominated durable goods industries. It would be asking a lot of state and local taxes, as an industry locational factor, to effect a greater *absolute* increase in metal or machinery workers in low-tax Alabama than was occurring in high-tax New York. But by substituting *rate* of growth of employment as the measure of growth, any bias that might be present favors Alabama.[14]

But the results of this second run with the tax factor do not warrant

---

[14] Although it has already been established that neither of the two tax variables harbor any inherent mechanical bias toward positive correlation, expressed as they are as ratios, a kind of ecological bias (?) may exist. A manufacturing economy ordinarily requires more government services (and taxes) than, say, an agricultural economy—probably both in absolute terms and as a share of total activity. It might be quite normal, therefore, for a high-tax (high manufacturing employment) state to add *more workers* than a low-tax (low manufacturing employment) state—but not to grow at a faster *rate*.

making any major change in the earlier conclusion. State and local taxes as a percent of personal income (the old variable X_7, unchanged) exhibits just one statistically significant correlation coefficient—and positive at that. The more refined form, state and local taxes per non-agricultural employee (the old X_8, unchanged) exhibits a statistically significant, negative correlation in apparel ($-.44$). (The tobacco coefficient $-.40$ falls short of statistical significance because it is derived from only fourteen observations; the required coefficient at the .05 level is .53.) Only in the apparel industry, then, has a *measurable* adverse tax effect been uncovered—a statistically significant, explained variance of 19 per cent.

The word "measurable" was chosen advisedly, our analytical device—correlation—is only a moderately sensitive instrument. To stay within a limit of only a five in one hundred chance of imputing significance to a chance result, only simple correlation coefficients of .28 or greater in the first model (with forty-nine observations) and of an even greater level in this second model (with its lesser observations) can be accepted as meaningful, *per se*. (Although lower coefficients may achieve significance in multiple regression equations in an additive role.) Using the first model as an illustration, with a .28 simple correlation coefficient adopted as minimal, anything less than 8 per cent association between taxes and growth can not be firmly established. That is to say, if taxes are a 5 per cent locational factor, this fact could not be established, at least not with so small a sample as forty-nine observations, within the framework of simple correlation—that is, taking taxes by themselves.

Another consideration which, perhaps, should serve as a restraint on the too quick drawing of hard and fast conclusions about the locational significance of taxes at the state level is the fact that the period under study was one of postwar boom when unusually strong expansionary forces (e.g., the wartime expansion of the money supply and the backlog demand for durables) may have literally swept before their force what would normally have been effective restraints on industrial growth (e.g., high business taxes). And, to repeat, none of these judgments warrants automatic extension to narrower industrial classes or intrastate industrial migration patterns. Still, in the final analysis, the existence, at the state level, of an appreciable tax effect on either the total amount or rate of employment growth in manufacturing remains as elusive, not to say illusory, as ever.

Labor Market Characteristics

Wage rates (X_9) and degree of unionization (X_{10}), two other strong contenders for the position of the most controversial facet of the local business climate, picked up their earlier trends by again exhibiting significant negative correlations in a number of non-durable goods industries, particularly, food, apparel, furniture and leather. In contrast to taxes, then, modest evidence is in hand that wage rates and/or the stage of unionization are sometimes important growth (locational) factors; the labor market and not the tax rate stands out as the more significant facet of the local business climate. Now, the question could quite properly be raised as to whether the rate-of-growth bias against bigness isn't at issue here. The fact remains, however, that the adverse wage-union effects show through primarily in the realm of the non-durables wherein the south is relatively closer to the north in employment size and is, therefore growing from a larger (less small) base than usual. But more convincing, it is hard to deny the evidence of an inverse correlation between the price and/or the nature of the labor supply, on the one hand, and subsequent employment growth in food, textiles, apparel and furniture, on the other hand, when such evidence is recorded for *both variables* ($X_{9, 10}$) in *both variants* (*Y* and *Y'*) of the model. While causation can not be established—only inferred—from correlation, the evidence strongly suggests a tendency for food, textile, apparel and furniture firms to seek low-wage, non-union labor markets and to do so *to a degree appreciably affecting both the absolute growth and the rate of growth in employment* in these four industries at the state level. This conclusion is, of course, not only not surprising but quite consistent with the many off-hand observations and individual case studies made of locational trends in these four foot-loose industries.

Educational Levels and Facilities

The three education variables (X'_{11}, X'_{12} and X'_{13}) provide a near classic case in the complexities and hazards of correlation analysis. A quick review of the simple correlation coefficients tying educational levels and facilities to manufacturing employment growth rates discloses the lack of even a single, statistically significant coefficient among the durable goods industries and precious few among the non-durables—half of which are negative (that is, probably derivative rather than causal in association). In fact, from this sample of sixty correlation coefficients, the few that are statistically significant barely exceed the number (three) which probably would have arisen due to pure chance—in a sample drawn from a zero correlation population. But, then, these are not sixty random coefficients; the durable goods industries reveal a preponderance of *low* positive correlations and the non-durables are similarly dominated by *weak* inverse associations between education and growth rate. And, surprisingly, the education variables enter the rate-of-growth estimating equations of fabricated metals (X_{11}, median school years), chemicals and all manufacturing (X'_{12}, per cent college graduates) and rubber and non-electrical machinery (X'_{13}, per cent college faculty). In each case, the education variable is the additive (second string) variable, accounting for about one-third of the explained variance with surprising consistency.

Thus, while the association between the educational level and facilities of a state and the subsequent rate of growth of manufacturing employment in that state appears not to be so strong as to dominate the pattern of growth, our results more than just suggest that education plays a significant additive role in all manufacturing and at least three sub-classes thereof. The fact that the influence of education on employment growth rates is exposed to view only after the effect of stronger, companion variables has been neutralized serves as a reminder that other *apparently innocuous* factors (even taxes) should not be written off as growth determinants too quickly—indeed, nothing can be unreservedly written off solely on the basis of correlation results.

Correlation Results: Multi-variate Analysis

Following earlier practice, the simple correlation coefficients were combined and re-combined into various groupings in an effort to formulate that equation which best fits and, hopefully, best explains the observed pattern of employment growth in each of the various manufacturing industries. In general, the multiple correlation coefficients were lower in this latter, rate-of-growth, variant than they were in the earlier, absolute-growth, formulation. But while this latter set of multiple correlations was well below the level of performance achieved earlier with reference to the durable goods industries, the rate-of-growth associations were nearly as close among the non-durables. (But, considering how modest were the achievements above in the non-durable goods sector, this is hardly a resounding victory; a break-through in the non-durables is still to come, probably awaiting, among other factors, the integration of resource-endowment variables.) That the rate-of-growth employment estimating equations should turn out as well as they did is quite surprising—in light of the host of low simple correlation coefficients from which these equations were fashioned. Formally, the explanation lies in the fact that the independent variables are not as closely correlated with each other in this variant of the model; that is, the explanatory powers of the independent variables, while separately slight, proved to be less duplicative and redundant, more

Table 12. Equations for Estimating Rate of Change in Employment in Selected Major Manufacturing Industry Groups, by States, 1947-54*

Food:
$$Y'_{20} = 0.5244 + \underset{(.1692)}{\overset{(.4354)}{0.5551}} X'_1 - \underset{(.01256)}{\overset{(-.6942)}{0.06570}} X_9 \pm 0.0142 \qquad R = .65$$

Tobacco:
$$Y'_{21} = 1.0014 + \underset{(.0000614)}{\overset{(.4805)}{0.0001321}} X'_5 - \underset{(.03766)}{\overset{(-.4163)}{0.07013}} X_9 \pm 0.0286 \qquad R = .68$$

Textiles:
$$Y'_{22} = 0.3097 + \underset{(.2768)}{\overset{(.3619)}{0.5920}} X'_2 - \underset{(.0001892)}{\overset{(-.2940)}{0.0003288}} X_8 \pm 0.0321 \qquad R = .55$$

Apparel:
$$Y'_{23} = 1.9984 - \underset{(.2420)}{\overset{(-.4523)}{0.8037}} X'_3 - \underset{(.03695)}{\overset{(-.2471)}{0.06704}} X_9 - \underset{(.005544)}{\overset{(-.2280)}{0.009828}} X'_{44} \pm 0.0434 \quad R = .62$$

Furniture:
$$Y'_{25} = 1.1689 - \underset{(0.300)}{\overset{(-.4869)}{0.1074}} X_9 - \underset{(.01409)}{\overset{(-.1878)}{0.01941}} X'_{46} \pm 0.0372 \qquad R = .53$$

Printing:
$$Y'_{27} = 0.6070 + \underset{(.1339)}{\overset{(.4077)}{0.5111}} X'_1 - \underset{(.000945)}{\overset{(-.4811)}{0.003823}} X_{10} - \underset{(.00383)}{\overset{(-.3944)}{0.01270}} X'_{48} \pm 0.0121 \quad R = .77$$

Chemicals:
$$Y'_{28} = -0.9275 + \underset{(.4130)}{\overset{(.5465)}{1.6739}} X'_2 + \underset{(.00733)}{\overset{(.2011)}{0.01094}} X'_{12} \pm 0.0587 \qquad R = .55$$

Petroleum:
$$Y'_{29} \equiv 0.6089 + \underset{(.1216)}{\overset{(.3660)}{0.3652}} X'_2 - \underset{(.00517)}{\overset{(-.5981)}{0.02539}} X'_{50} \pm 0.0172 \qquad R = .66$$

Rubber:
$$Y'_{30} = 1.0718 - \underset{(.001491)}{\overset{(-.4714)}{0.003058}} X_{10} + \underset{(.00866)}{\overset{(.2880)}{0.01086}} X'_{13} \pm 0.0189 \qquad R = .64$$

Stone, clay & glass:
$$Y'_{32} = 1.2771 + \underset{(.1406)}{\overset{(.4790)}{1.0158}} X'_1 - \underset{(.0877)}{\overset{(-.7916)}{1.0744}} X'_2 - \underset{(.000200)}{\overset{(-.6691)}{0.002088}} X_{10} \pm 0.0122 \quad R = .92$$

Fabricated metals:
$$Y'_{34} = -0.0920 + \underset{(.3014)}{\overset{(.4420)}{0.9377}} X'_2 + \underset{(.005336)}{\overset{(.1851)}{0.008154}} X_{11} - \underset{(.00421)}{\overset{(-.3117)}{0.01066}} X'_{55} \pm 0.0383 \quad R = .67$$

Machinery, except electrical:
$$Y'_{35} = 0.0646 + \underset{(.2651)}{\overset{(.4387)}{0.8347}} X'_2 - \underset{(.0006032)}{\overset{(-.2244)}{0.0009815}} X_{10} + \underset{(.00899)}{\overset{(.2505)}{0.01624}} X'_{13} \pm 0.0380 \quad R = .54$$

Electrical machinery:
$$Y'_{36} = 1.17766 + \underset{(.0000708)}{\overset{(.4499)}{0.0001891}} X'_5 - \underset{(.001642)}{\overset{(-.4618)}{0.004500}} X_{10} \pm 0.0583 \qquad R = .62$$

All manufacturing:
$$Y'_{40} = 0.6795 + \underset{(.1744)}{\overset{(.3943)}{0.4813}} X'_2 + \underset{(.002165)}{\overset{(.3919)}{0.008493}} X'_{12} - \underset{(.003192)}{\overset{(-.3983)}{0.008984}} X'_{60} \pm 0.0175 \quad R = .79$$

Table 12—Continued

where:

Y':   Estimated annual rate of change in total employment in the state, 1947–54;

X_1':   Annual rate of change in state population, 1940–47;

X_2':   Annual rate of change in state personal income, 1940–47;

X_3':   Annual rate of change in state personal income, 1945–48;

X_5':   Expenditures for new plant and equipment in all manufacturing industries per manufacturing employee, by states, 1947;

X_8:   Estimated state and local taxes paid by non-agricultural business per employee, by states, 1953;

X_9:   Average hourly earnings in manufacturing industries, by states, 1949;

X_{10}:   Estimated trade union membership as a per cent of non-agricultural employment, by states, 1947;

X_{11}:   Median years of school completed by persons twenty-five years old and over, by states, 1950;

X_{12}':   Per cent of persons twenty-five years old and over who have completed four or more years of college, by states, 1950;

X_{13}':   Total staff at institutions of higher education (1947–48) as a per cent of persons twenty-five years old and over (1950), by states;

X_{44}':   Employment (1947) in apparel and related products as a per cent of total employment (1950), by states;

X_{46}':   Employment (1947) in furniture and fixtures as a per cent of total employment (1950), by states;

X_{48}':   Employment (1947) in printing and publishing as a per cent of total employment (1950), by states;

X_{50}':   Employment (1947) in petroleum and coal products as a per cent of total employment (1950), by states;

X_{55}':   Employment (1947) in fabricated metal products as a per cent of total employment (1950), by states;

X_{60}':   Employment (1947) in all manufacturing as a per cent of total employment (1950), by states.

* *The figure in parentheses below the regression coefficient is the standard error of the coefficient in original units, and the figure above is the regression coefficient in standard units.*

additive, than before.[15] The rate-of-growth employment estimating equations for fourteen of the twenty major industry groups are set forth in Table 12.

Although not quite matching its performance in the absolute-growth construct, the growth of the local market again stands out as a prime locational factor in manufacturing industries, with its appearance as one

[15] Also, there is the important advantage of low inter-correlation (low multicollinearity) in multiple correlation analysis in that the separate effect of a particular variable can be isolated with greater confidence. More reliable estimates of regression coefficients can be made because these coefficients tend to be more stable as other variables are added to or deleted from the equation.

of the variables in nine out of fourteen of the best estimating equations. In point of distinction, however, the annual rate of change in personal income, 1940–47, (X_2') holds a clear advantage over the annual rate of change in population, 1940–47 (X_1') as the precursor of subsequent employment growth in manufacturing, reversing their relative positions in the earlier results. At almost every turn of the study the leading role of local demand as a stimulus to further industrialization has asserted itself undeniably.

The pattern takes a turn with reference to the labor market variables; wage rates and union strength play a much stronger role in the present rate-of-growth model. Again, the apparel and furniture industry equations include average hourly earnings (X_9), with the wage rate influence relatively strongest in furniture. But, while the evidence grows that low wages spur employment growth in these two industries, it must not be forgotten that only about 30 per cent of the interstate growth variations in apparel and furniture are explained by our equations (in either the absolute or rate-of-growth variants) and of this amount only about one-half can be attributed to wage rates. Low wage rates apparently also foreshadow a high rate of employment growth in two other non-durables, food and tobacco manufacturing.

The companion variable to wage rates, union membership as a per cent of the non-agricultural labor force (X_{10}), is a (negative) factor in the best estimate of the employment growth rate in two non-durables, printing and rubber products manufacturing. The degree of unionization is the leading variable of the three which combine to produce for the printing industry the best statistical fit achieved among the non-durables—explained variance of 59 per cent. This rough measure of union strength is, moreover, the dominant variable in the rubber products equation. More surprisingly, however, a high degree of unionism is also associated with low rates of employment growth in two durable goods industries. In stone, clay and glass manufacturing, the per cent of the labor market unionized accounts for a little over one-third of the variance explained by the estimating equation in which it is incorporated; this is made somewhat more significant by the fact that the stone-clay-glass equation attains the highest correlation of the rate-of-growth set—an explained variance of 85 per cent. Unionization (negative) and all manufacturing investment (positive) share the limelight in the electrical machinery equation, jointly accounting for 38 per cent explained variance. This same variable also appears in the equation for estimating state rates of growth in employment in fabricated metal products but, considering that it is the least of three variables, which together only account for about 29 per cent of the variance to be explained, its status here is too weak and uncertain to stress.

The degree of local specialization (X_{41-60}') enters the best employment estimating equation for six of the industry groups: apparel, furniture, printing, petroleum, fabricated metal and the aggregate of all manufacturing. Thus, the constraint that past development of an industry has on the current rate of growth of that industry is significant enough to suggest predictive value for this variable in a number of industries. Further, the weight of this variable compares very favorably with that of its companion variables in the various equations.

State and local business taxes per employee enter the apparel employment estimating equation, but this is the first and only appearance of either tax variable in any of our multiple regression equations.

V

GUIDEPOSTS TO THE SECOND APPROXIMATION

Nothing could be more gratuitous at this juncture than the customary disclaimer accompanied by the conventional stricture that much remains to be done. Promising avenues deserving of further exploration are so many and so suggestive that the opportunities are bewildering. A half dozen directions in which this study could be extended have already been suggested in the foregoing text, or at least implied.

While the index of industrial development has already been expressed in two forms, absolute growth and rate of growth of employment, further variants demand consideration. As against our current preoccupation with these measures of size, some index of productivity such as value added per employee or per capita income might be adopted to reflect efficiency or performance. This possibility was brought out in the analysis of the education variables in Chapter II as one limitation of the model.

A second limitation is that by being restricted to manufacturing activity we ignored an appreciable—perhaps even critical—amount of basic economic activity. Since this regional growth analysis ignores agriculture, mining and transportation, financial and tourist services, can it be seriously assumed that Iowa, Utah, Illinois, New York and Florida are fully represented?

In addition to the need for greater industrial breadth, a finer industrial disaggregation might reveal patterns lost in the welter of heterogeneous averaging. It will be recalled that the attempt to formulate an employment estimating equation for stone, clay and glass manufacturing seemed to indicate a blurring due to excessive industrial aggregation. And the separable industrial identities of automobile, aircraft, locomotive and ship building, presently lumped together as transportation equipment manufacturing, need not be labored. Data limitations are, of course, the first hurdle here; but a beginning could be made by building up from state and local data for a few selected areas.

Perhaps most damaging of all, no systematic analyses of the relevant time series has yet been made; the leads and lags assumed are a product of the roughest kind of guesses and hunches. The magnitude of this task suggests that it would be advisable to select just a few "industries" and to analyze their time series over a much longer period than the one employed here. Closely allied with the objective of establishing the timing of the functional relationship with greater precision is the clear need to define the pattern of causation more rigorously—to separate exogenous from endogenous forces. Population growth, for example, is closely followed by employment growth in all manufacturing and many sub-varieties thereof. But which came first: the population chicken or the manufacturing-employment egg? Only by extending the time horizon can this question be answered, or at least attacked. Or, again, only through time series analysis can we hope to make progress toward defining the seemingly ambivalent role of average hourly earnings; through time series analysis we may be able to carefully distinguish between the (apparently) exogenous role of wage rates in apparel and furniture employment growth and the (apparently) endogenous role of wage rates in the growth of the durables.

Last but not least—and maybe even first—the spatial dimension of growth is lacking. In common with all too many regional analyses, this study has been spaceless in concept and content; no direct reference has been made to the locations of the various states—their positions in space relative to each other. Spatial relationships are too often ignored in economic analysis, probably due in large measure to the fact that spatial patterns (as distinct from distances) are difficult to quantify. While a spaceless *first* approximation of the pattern of regional industrial development may be defended on the pragmatic grounds of simplicity and ease of quantification, recourse to maps, location theory and spatial measurement should achieve a respectable niche in the second approximation—difficulties encountered in matters of concept and measurement notwithstanding.

ADDENDUM TO CHAPTER V

A MODEST STEP TOWARD THAT SECOND APPROX-IMATION: THE SPATIAL DIMENSION

While neither the time nor the resources were at hand for us to proceed with a systematic inquiry into even one of the many avenues of promise outlined above, we attempted some tentative probings into the spatial dimension of regional industrial development. What follows is little more than a set of working papers, but ones which, at the least, may interest and, more hopefully, may stimulate other students of regional economic development.

The Propensity to Migrate

Almost invariably, the regional economic analyst is confronted with the two-part question: which are the more locationally-mobile (foot-loose) industries and which have been the more migratory ones? Surprisingly little of a comprehensive nature has been done on this score. With data which came to hand as a by-product of our main line of inquiry, we developed an index of the migratory character of the various manufacturing industries and computed the relevant values for the period 1947–54. Following this, we depicted the spatial pattern of industrial migration in a series of maps in the hope (already partly fulfilled) that further insight would be gained into recent trends in state industrial development.

The technique employed to isolate recent trends in the relocation of manufacturing was simple and direct.

1. Each state's fractional share of the national employment in a major industry group was computed for the year 1947, then

2. These state market shares were applied to the 1954 national employment in that industry, yielding the amount of that kind of employment which each state would have had in 1954 if it had maintained its old (1947) market share, then

3. These hypothetical employments were subtracted from the actual 1954 employments in that industry, state by state, yielding positive and negative changes in employment which reflect the number of jobs won from or lost to other states.

To illustrate, application of the technique to Michigan's share of the printing and publishing industry yields the following result:

$$26,973 \quad - \quad (.03031 \quad \times \quad 804,386) \quad = \quad +2,592$$

| Michigan's actual employment in that industry in in 1954 | Michigan's share of national employ- ment in that in- dustry in 1947 | National employ- ment in that in- dustry in 1954 | Number of jobs "won" from other states be- tween 1947 and 1954 |

Michigan's hypothetical employment in that indus- try in 1954 (= 24,381)

The Magnitude of Industrial Relocation

As a point of departure, some overall impression of the relative magnitude of industrial migration will provide a surer feeling for the detail (of the maps) which follows. In Table 13 the various Census-defined, major industry groups are ranked by two distinct measures of locational shift. On the left hand side of the table an *absolute* measure is employed: *number of jobs shifted* from one state to another. Thus, for the transportation equipment industry, 292,700 workers were employed in 1954 in states other than the ones in which they would have been employed if each state had maintained its 1947 share of that industry in 1954.[16] On the right hand side a *relative* measure is employed: the number of jobs shifted as a per cent of the 1954 employment in that industry. Thus, the 292,700 transportation equipment workers employed at locations not in conformance with the 1947 locational pattern for that industry accounted for 17.2 per cent of the total national employment in that industry in 1954.

Even the most cursory examination of the *absolute* form of the index (left hand side of Table 13) reveals a tremendous range in the amount of job migration between the various industries. Transportation equipment exhibits an interstate shift in the number of jobs of almost sixty times that of tobacco manufactures, the least of the group. In *relative* terms, however, transportation equipment manufacturing exhibits only about five times as great a degree of relocation as does food and kindred products manufacturing, the most locationally stable of the group. The explanation of this sharp divergence in internal variation of the two indexes is that a measure expressed in absolute terms reflects the size of the industry: clearly tobacco, with a total national employment of only about 95,000

---

[16] See the dagger footnote to Table 13.

in 1954 could not have matched the absolute shift in jobs taking place in the giant transportation equipment industry (over 1,700,000 employed nationally in 1954), even if every tobacco job had shifted to a theretofore non-tobacco state.

But good cause can be elicited to support the use of an absolute measure which reflects the employment weights of the respective industries to which it is applied; for many, perhaps most, purposes it is the *number* of job opportunities won or lost upon which regional well-being rests, not percentage changes. Unquestionably, transportation equipment qualifies as the industry which had the most pronounced effect on the geographical redistribution of manufacturing employment which occurred during the

Table 13. *The Number and Per Cent of Manufacturing Workers Employed in 1954 in States Other than the Ones in Which They Would Have Been Employed if the 1947 Market Shares of the Various States Had Been Maintained through to 1954**

Absolute Index of Interstate Industrial Migration			Relative Index of Interstate Industrial Migration		
Rank	Major industry group	Number of jobs shifted†	Rank	Major industry group	Per cent of jobs shifted†
1	Transportation equipment	292,700	1	Transportation equipment	17.2
2	Textile-mill products	109,200	2	Textile-mill products	10.5
3	Apparel & related products	81,100	3	Instruments & related products	9.8
4	Electrical machinery	78,600	4	Chemicals & allied products	9.7
5	Machinery, except electrical	77,100	5	Lumber & related products	9.1
6	Chemicals & allied products	71,600	6	Electrical machinery	8.2
7	Fabricated metal products	63,900	7	Furniture & fixtures	7.4
8	Lumber & related products	51,800	8	Apparel & related products	6.8
9	Food & kindred products	48,700	9	Rubber products	6.6
10	Primary metal industries	47,900	10	Paper & allied products	6.4
11	Paper & allied products	34,100	11	Fabricated metal products	6.3
12	Printing & publishing	33,100	12	Leather & leather products	5.8
13	Stone, clay, & glass products	27,900	13	Stone, clay, & glass products	5.7
14	Instrument & related products	26,600	14	Tobacco manufactures	5.2
15	Furniture & fixtures	25,300	15	Machinery, except electrical	5.0
16	Leather & leather products	20,600	16	Petroleum & coal products	5.0
17	Rubber products	16,200	17	Primary metal industries	4.3
18	Petroleum & coal products	10,600	18	Printing & publishing	4.1
19	Tobacco manufactures	5,000	19	Food & kindred products	3.6
	Total (gross)	1,124,000			
	All manufacturing (net)	704,500		All manufacturing (net)	4.5

* *Derived from Department of Commerce, Bureau of the Census, Census of Manufactures: 1947 and 1954 (Washington: 1950 and 1957).*

† *The term "shifted" does not necessarily imply an actual migration of workers or even of job opportunities. If the total employment in an industry is unchanged between two years, then any change in state market shares of that industry will entail an actual migration of jobs (and perhaps also workers). But in a growing industry a shift in the locational pattern could occur simply by having all or most of the employment gain go to one or a few states with no state losing even a single job. Similarly, regionally disproportionate contraction will shift the industry locational pattern even though no jobs (or workers) disappear in one state and turn up in another.*

period 1947–1954. The lead of this industry is a commanding one indeed, accounting as it does for nearly three times as much job migration as the runner-up, textile-mill products, and for slightly over one-quarter of the total (gross[17]) shift in manufacturing employment. Textile-mill products, probably the most publicized industrial migrant of recent years, runs a poor second but still holds a sizable lead over the rest of the pack, which follow each other closely.

On first blush, it is probably a little surprising to find heavy industry (e.g., metals, machinery, vehicles) so well represented at the top of the list. The very term "heavy" seems to connote not only a large capital investment (and large fixed costs) but also a kind of spatial immobility, even a kind of spatial determinateness—the converse of being foot-loose. But then, of course, an industry may change its locational pattern without any physical movement of facilities whatsoever—if California adds automobile workers while Michigan's automobile employment holds steady, the industry's locational pattern shifts westward even though not a single worker or machine is spatially displaced. Moreover, it is these same heavy industries which are the largest employers and, consequently, even a small relative change becomes a large absolute magnitude. This conclusion is supported by a comparison of the rank order of the various industries when the relative form of the industrial migration index is substituted for the absolute form. Transportation equipment excepted, the heavy industries slip sharply in position to an overall rank of slightly below median.

Of interest, but quite in line with expectations, the natural-resource-based industries show the greatest relative stability of locational pattern. Food products manufacturing with the smallest relative shift (3.6 per cent) is closely followed by primary metals (4.3 per cent), petroleum (5.0 per cent), tobacco (5.2 per cent), and stone, clay and glass (5.7 per cent); this farm-and-mine oriented group accounts for five out of the last seven positions. Lumber (9.1 per cent) and chemicals (9.7 per cent), less clearly a member of the resource-based family of industries, provide the major exceptions to the tendency for the raw-material-processing industries to exhibit the most stable locational patterns. There does not appear to be any systematic relationship between the durability of a product and the propensity of that industry to migrate; durable and non-durable goods are randomly distributed when ranked by *per cent* of employment shifted (the relative form of the index).

[17] The sum of the number of job shifts for the nineteen industries is larger than the figure for all manufacturing because the latter is a net figure, that is, one in which locational shifts in the sub-groups may offset one another. For example, North Carolina's "loss" of 1,393 tobacco manufacturing workers must be offset against her "gain" of 1,553 printing and publishing workers, largely cancelling out both magnitudes.

In subsequent analyses, these two indexes would probably be best employed in separate and distinct contexts. In its *absolute* form the index would seem to be most useful as a tool of regional analysis; in its *relative* form, the index would seem to be more appropriate as a tool of location theory. The growth and decline of regions is in part a matter of sheer numbers and the locational trends of big industries should weigh more heavily than those of small industries. Sheer size is an important fact of and force in economic life. Conversely, inquiries into the forces and the processes (as distinct from the impact) of industrial migration lead the analyst to regard each industry as a case study of cause and effect, any one of which, big or small, may reveal critical locational factors. Thus, any inter-industry comparisons employed to reveal patterns of locational behavior need not, indeed ordinarily should not, accord separate observations (industries) different weights, depending on their respective employments.

The Pattern of Industrial Relocation

The most immediate use to which this analysis of industrial migration might be put is to further refine employment estimating equations. Adopting a relative form of the industrial-migration index to depict changing locational patterns, we constructed a map for each of the twenty manufacturing industry groups showing each state's gain or loss in market share of employment. In Figures 1 to 20 which follow, each + represents a state gain of two-tenths of one per cent (0.2 per cent) of the total (1947) employment in the given industry and each 0 represents the loss in state market share of a like amount. However, a systematic review of the maps which follow has yet to be undertaken. But the value of the transportation equipment industry map has already been established (Chap. III) and this case alone suggests that further spatial analysis deserves a high priority in subsequent research efforts—and that these industry-migration maps may be profitably employed as a point of departure.

VI

SUMMARY OF FINDINGS

This is the report of a pilot study undertaken to explore the nature of
state industrial development, with special emphasis on some first approximations to estimating equations with which employment growth trends
might be predicted. We have designed an econometric model of simple
form, embracing twenty varieties of manufacturing activity, forty-eight
states, and the years 1947–1954. Specifically, this is an (interstate) cross-
section, multiple correlation and regression analysis of (seven-year) employment trends. We estimated employment growth by fitting a least
squares trend line to annual employment data drawn from the 1947 and
the 1954 *Census of Manufactures* and the 1949 to 1953 *Annual Survey of
Manufactures*. Average annual change in employment, our index of industrial development (the dependent variable), was then correlated with a
number of potential determinants of growth (independent variables);
these correlation coefficients were then combined and re-combined to
produce the best employment estimating equation for each of the industry
groups.

The principal findings are:

1. Durable goods industries exhibit growth patterns which are easier
to explain than non-durables. While all of the independent variables
except the tax and labor market indexes are closely associated with interstate differentials in durable goods growth patterns, time and again, the
analysis of regional trends in the non-durables seemed to founder on the
need for some natural-resource-supply variable—the food, tobacco, textile,
lumber, chemical and petroleum industries, for example. Further study of
these farm-and-mine-oriented industries would seem to call for the integration into our model of the lessons of economic geography. Paper and
printing are the major exceptions to this rule, being non-durables that
behave more like durables.

2. Perhaps the single most important finding of the study is that of the
key role played by the growth of the local market. Prior state population
and income changes (1940–47) statistically explain from one-quarter to
four-fifths of interstate differentials in employment growth of the various
durable goods industries and nine-tenths of the variance between states
in all manufacturing employment. But, excepting paper and printing
which behave throughout very much like durables, the non-durables

apparently were not appreciably attracted to the booming (city) markets, reflecting, in part, their stronger natural resource orientation (especially, food, tobacco, lumber, petroleum). Still to be established, of course, is which came first: the population chicken or the manufacturing-employment egg. Clearly, further analysis of the pattern of leads and lags is now in order to establish the direction of causation or, at least, chronological sequence.

3. There is strong evidence that industrialization begets further in-dustrialization in a kind of locational variant on the acceleration-effect theme. Prior growth in total manufacturing employment (1939–47) is closely linked with subsequent growth in employment in the basic metal, machine, vehicle and instrument industries. This is, of course, not too surprising because the growth of practically any and all types of manu-facturing could be reasonably expected to elicit an expansion of local sup-porting industries—especially these capital goods suppliers.

4. Related to this result, as a by-product of the main line of inquiry, we uncovered evidence which indicates that the durable goods (and, in large measure, capital goods) industries tend to grow in locational linkage— tend toward spatial agglomeration in growth. No such tendency is evident among the non-durables or between durables and non-durables. Fabricated metal products, especially, seems to be an integral part of the development of these heterogeneous durable goods complexes, with roughly half of the interstate variation in the employment growth of the other durables as-sociated with a corresponding amount of change in fabricated metal em-ployment. While employment in fabricated metals may not be the key to the growth of a durable goods complex, it seems often to be the core. Conversely, the locational patterns of durables and non-durables seem either to be unrelated, as when raw material requirements diverge, or to be repellent, as when non-durables can not meet the competition of the durables in the labor market (food, textile, leather and rubber growth patterns are negatively correlated with the development of the durables, more often than not). The various non-durables seem to follow unrelated regional growth patterns.

5. Expenditures for new plant and equipment (the supply of productive capacity) are not nearly as reliable a harbinger of subsequent trends in employment as one might expect, a priori. But investment in lumber, paper, chemicals and primary metals plant and equipment was correlated with employment growth in those industries—and sufficiently so to give promise of having predictive value. Somewhat surprisingly, the aggregate of all manufacturing plant and equipment expenditures was much more closely correlated with the subsequent growth in six of the seven durable goods industries than were their individual industry investment series.

All manufacturing investment is, moreover, a variable in the instrument industry employment estimating equation, probably reflecting the influence of any and all kinds of investment on the *demand* for locally made instruments.

6. Total patent grants issued to residents, the most novel of the independent variables, proved to be a sensitive enough indicator of subsequent employment growth in the electrical machinery, instruments, and stone, clay and glass industries to win a place in the best employment estimating equation for those industries. Moreover, expressed in a more selective form, chemistry patent grants anticipate chemical employment growth sufficiently well to enter the estimating equation for that industry; while metallurgical, metal working, turning and gear cutting, and internal combustion engine patent grants almost made the primary metal, fabricated metal, non-electrical machinery and transportation equipment equations, respectively. In that there is ample room in which to improve the patent indexes used, our experience has been such as to tempt us to invest further in this ambitious attempt to quantify technology as a regional growth factor.

7. State and local tax differentials, whether expressed more generally as a per cent of state income or more specifically as taxes paid by business per employee, appear to have no measurable effect on interstate differentials in employment growth in any of the twenty manufacturing industry groups. (Only locational forces accounting for 8 per cent or more of the observed interstate growth differentials can be "measured"—statistically established—with a forty-eight state sample.) The presumption is that either government provides a rough *quid pro quo* of services in return for taxes paid or that state and local taxes are relatively unimportant costs of doing business. But these results in no way prejudice the question of the tax sensitivity of narrower industry classes than the ones adopted or the *intra*state locational effects of local tax differentials.

8. Low wage rates are associated with rapid employment growth in food, leather, primary metals and, especially, apparel and furniture; but only in the latter two was the apparent dampening effect of high wage rates and stimulating effect of low wage rates sufficiently strong to give promise of important predictive properties. And, in sharp contrast to this, six of the seven durable goods industries grew faster in the higher wage rate areas, indicating, of course, not that high wages attract, but that industrial development effects high wages. This kind of about-face from negative to positive correlation suggests, again, the need for further analysis to define the characteristic lines of causation that link wage rates and employment growth.

9. The variable expressing the per cent of labor force unionized behaves

much as expected: a few modest inverse correlations among the non-durables (food, leather, and apparel, statistically significant, and textiles and furniture, very nearly so) and positive coefficients of comparable level for six of the seven durables. Thus, analogous to wage rates, unions exert a mild repelling effect on about half of the foot-loose, lower skilled, non-durable goods industries, while the less mobile, skill demanding durables appear to thrive in highly unionized labor markets (with unionization probably being the dependent variable, again). However, such influence as this variable exerts on growth is too weak to accord it a role in any of the employment estimating equations.

10. With respect to the role of education, median-school-years-completed, surprisingly, is significantly associated with only one of the twenty industry groups (lumber). While it is much too early to write off the overall level of formal education of the labor force as a determinant of state industrial development, these results at least suggest that a mass-education index which will prove useful in either an explanatory or predictive role will probably not be easily assembled. Conversely, the number of college-educated persons shows a close correlation with the durable goods industries, with a median explained variance of about 50 per cent. This correlation pattern is almost exactly duplicated by the supply-of-college-faculty variable. But neither variable is much better than the correlation results which can be obtained by simply using total population for the same year. The inference here is that emphasis on higher education in an area does not portend a rapid growth of jobs but rather of the "better" jobs—our dependent variable is too gross in nature. If, however, the growth of state per capita income or value added per worker were the dependent variable instead, the education variables would probably pull well ahead of a population variable as a growth force.

11. Area employment in the industry in 1947—base year employment—displays a pattern of correlation coefficients which suggests the generalization that the existing durable goods centers tend to fatten their leads, while a mixed tendency prevails among the non-durables. In general, "locational inertia" seems to build up more often than not and, quite rationally, it appears to be most characteristic of industries with heavy fixed investments and complex technologies (e.g., metals, machinery and tools plus paper and oil). But sheer size is still a lesser force in determining the absolute amount of industrial change to follow than would probably have been presumed, *a priori*.

By converting absolute changes to rates of change and absolute numbers to ratios, the model was re-run as a rate-of-growth variant. Further findings are:

12. The (rate of) growth of the local market still stands out as a prime industry locational factor, although it is less dominant now and, in turn-

about, personal income edges population for the stellar role. Of the fourteen estimating equations reported in rate-of-change form, one of these two indexes of local market demand appears in all but five: tobacco, apparel, furniture, rubber and electrical machinery (each of which, interestingly, is measurably oriented toward low-wage-rate and/or less-unionized labor markets).

13. Wage rates and the degree of unionization of the local labor force now play much more prominent roles: low wage rates are linked with rapid rates of employment growth in (again) apparel and furniture and (newly) in food and tobacco manufacturing; the relatively non-union labor states experienced the highest employment growth rates in printing, rubber, electrical machinery, and stone, clay and glass manufacturing. Thus, integrating the findings here with above, low-wage-rate, non-union labor markets have been the fastest growing centers of food, textile, apparel and furniture manufacturing—regardless of whether an absolute or a relative measure of employment growth is adopted.

14. The rate of employment growth in textiles is inversely correlated with state and local business taxes per employee and sufficiently so to earn it a place in the best employment estimating equation for that industry; but this is the only significant association between taxes and employment growth evident in either the absolute or rate-of-growth variants of the model. So, apart from this single exception, the existence of a tax effect on either the absolute amount or rate of employment growth in manufacturing remains as elusive, not to say illusory, as ever.

15. The rate of growth of employment in apparel, furniture, printing, petroleum, fabricated metal and the aggregate of all manufacturing is inversely associated with the degree to which the local economy has already specialized in those industries, as measured by the per cent of local total employment engaged in those industries. And the correlations are close enough to place the degree-of-local-specialization variable in the best employment estimating equations for those industry groups. That (roughly) a high level of development should have a dampening effect on the current *rate* of development is a quite unsurprising conclusion to be sure. But that this inverse association between past and current rates of growth might be close enough to have a significant influence and, perhaps, predictive value is not patent.

16. Somewhat digressively, the transportation equipment industry was established as the industry in which the greatest (absolute and relative) amount of regional job shifting took place—the one contributing the most to the postwar relocation of manufacturing industry. Textiles were a distant second in rank, with no notable overall pattern of industrial migration readily apparent.

17. The analysis of regional job shifting did, however, emphasize the

spatial aspects of industrial development and suggest new avenues for further exploration. The "mapping" of regional differentials in the development of the transportation equipment industry, for example, indicated the need to enlarge the chosen areal unit of analysis (the state); some larger, multi-state region would conform more closely to that spatial pattern which is crystallizing—a multiple-nuclei pattern of decentralization.

APPENDIX A

DEPENDENT VARIABLES

Estimated average annual change in total employment and estimated annual rate of change in total employment by states, 1947–54, in major industry groups.

Table A-1, Estimated Average Annual Change in Total Employment in Manufacturing Industries, by States, 1947–54*

States	Food[a] Y_{20}	Tobacco Y_{21}	Textiles Y_{22}	Apparel Y_{23}	Lumber[b] Y_{24}	Furniture Y_{25}	Paper Y_{26}	Printing Y_{27}	Chemicals Y_{28}	Petroleum & coal Y_{29}	Rubber Y_{30}	Leather Y_{31}	Stone, clay & glass Y_{32}	Primary metal Y_{33}	Fabricated metal Y_{34}	Machinery Y_{35}	Electrical machinery Y_{36}	Transportation equipment Y_{37}	Instruments Y_{38}	All manufacturing Y_{40}
Maine	222	0	-1,081	-69	641	14	251	4	-16	0	0	722	16	-16	57	-423	0	76	0	1,038
New Hampshire	0	0	-518	-205	-167	87	80	98	-20	0	0	98	90	-1	66	148	0	0	191	1,208
Vermont	-2	0	-302	122	-139	-56	-105	37	-16	0	263	13	220	-3	16	528	0	0	0	691
Massachusetts	-901	-4	-7,303	1,409	-180	235	190	52	-222	-30		-278	96	252	46	-137	5,188	750	378	1,307
Rhode Island	-54	0	-2,110	169	-1	-29	-36	46	-3	0	-61	47	139	204	63		-33	0	104	-854
Connecticut	-20	0	-1,421	214	32	63	114	288	322	32	424	136	-74	-546	-706	1,551	882	6,276	-17	9,555
New York	-635	-141	-3,630	-718	93	116	587	28	320	-263	228	-926	253	1,580	2,212	4,122	5,963	9,386	875	31,675
New Jersey	1,083	-182	-2,292	1,232	120	231	560	750	376	228	-189	96	911	209	1,424	1,574	4,082	2,975	1,314	15,231
Pennsylvania	-1,471	-414	-5,170	706	-182	1,013	525	680	903	-96	157	-263	446	3,105	844	1,294	4,363	2,094	1,270	13,697
Ohio	-362	-195	406	-449	-18	-430	416	1,409	1,096	289	-469	-645	971	3,017	1,498	2,931	1,625	13,791	211	30,417
Indiana	-688	-68	-517	-257	328	40	95	246	1,338	-55	-15	-90	617	-20	647	1,752	4,000	5,002	26	15,848
Illinois	-1,663	-35	-122	-1,390	208	97	510	-665	605	117	163	-1,033	450	1,034	2,029	999	5,021	2,218	606	12,916
Michigan	-191	-36	-348	209	-591	61	658	494	803	131	-304	-45	412	-499	2,230	6,299	65	6,021	591	19,781
Wisconsin	-478	0	-536	-81	403	-139	749	435	678	24	-104	-473	0	553	-152	394	1,789	488	158	7,331
Minnesota	-681	0	-251	46	6	-6	607	150	62	19	6	-15	149	-204	57	417	-648	543	0	4,749
Iowa	76	0	0	-67	225	57	134	250	212	0	150	-27	118	374	246	1,775	636	275	187	4,165
Missouri	-956	0	68	-222	-208	-109	210	254	427	147	0	-761	15	178	643	470	885	3,668	128	9,703
North Dakota	-218	0	0	0	0	0	0	35		0	0	0	12	0	11	26	0	0	0	195
South Dakota	64	0	0	0	-23	0	0	38	-17	0	0	0	7	0	47	-26	0	0	0	131
Nebraska	-44	0	0	45	102	13	0	98	34	0	0	0	59	0	204	115	29	-69	0	1,812
Kansas	-957	0	0	41	44	-44	10	296	878	21	0	-1	238	-65	344	692	0	7,592	0	10,551
Delaware	40	0	-24	128	-61		3	63	-5	-2	0	-138	42	47	-102	26	0	272	0	1,168
Maryland	162	0	-327	391	122	260	207	210	-351	99	140	-85	89	413	160	305	848	2,615	10	6,502
District of Columbia	-157		0	-1	0	4	28	107	7				7	0	7	10	18	0	0	367
Virginia	434	-265	805	905	-870	187	127	298	882	0	73	-26	319	-67	355	135	0	817	64	5,287
West Virginia	-51	20	-164	90	-85	32	14	13	368	67	0	-123	-816	188	-152	122	175	0	34	125
North Carolina	351	-985	3,352	715	-1,243	1,061	258	321	304	0	0	-31	166	38	325	482	0	-32	116	9,948
South Carolina	52	-61	1,310	1,534	-268	10	10	118	2,468	0	0	0	167	-27	0	234	0	-76	0	5,283
Georgia	927	0	769	1,617	-1,871	314	806	261	-54	12	0	22	111	22	328	97	189	3,134	0	7,664
Florida	1,033	31	61	603	-852	429	828	479	810	40	0	56	420	84	684	202	113	101	0	6,970

Major industry group

Kentucky	-191	199	46	520	-378	-210	61	131	899	38	0	-132	77	-42	170	607	877	24	-26	3,554
Tennessee	-43	0	-245	1,420	-366	359	421	153	2,614	-19	-97	-44	37	-398	376	571	479	218	84	8,249
Alabama	143	0	-563	1,611	-1,293	74	512	99	-73	84	100	0	156	252	384	-161	0	595	0	3,114
Mississippi	16	0	-7	1,212	-61	288	606	54	129	0	0	0	63	-16	264	108	0	0	0	2,835
Arkansas	397	0	0	288	-540	300	115	70	265	34	314	37	-95	187	-234	0	28	0		2,637
Louisiana	-57	4	14	-378	11	404	97	663	237	0	189	520	89	227	0	-15	10			3,293
Oklahoma	-360	0	238	-57	69	28	100	0	-7	31	295	140	407	658	474	1,614	11			3,888
Texas	-107	76	1,116	-1,600	590	459	620	2,246	592	314	373	1,966	575	1,583	474	6,042	244			17,806
Montana	-44	0	0	419	0	35	65	0	-11	-20	-10	6	0	0	2	0	0			3,647
Idaho	53	0	0	501	0	-3	112	79	25	43	50	-12	0	0	12	0	0			1,191
Wyoming	-40	0	0	8	0	17	0	0	9	0	0	0	0	0	0					73
Colorado	-92	0	43	96	35	180	14	297	55	249	66	159	111	159	98	25	51			1,509
New Mexico	57	0	0	17	-4	46	0	883	0	0	69	0	7	0	0	0	0			1,238
Arizona	9	0	112	16	13	101	0	114	0	0	24	150	105	159	0	934	0			1,820
Utah	-40	-40	54	-5	-1	-16	0	79	73	0	52	284	162	114	32	0	0			973
Nevada	-31	0	0	22	-10	32	0	0	131	0	0	0	0	0	0				473
Washington	-552	7	159	584	-43	446	57	1,074	1	18	42	824	203	419	25	3,526	50			8,204
Oregon	-255	-48	91	2,879	-179	242	54	71	-7	-20	11	36	270	-1	80	-37	0			4,834
California	1,420	126	1,893	2,524	736	1,358	1,317	909	-37	71	1,033	1,790	3,785	3,347	6,772	28,577	1,065			63,645
United States	-7,741	-2,306	-20,548	14,621	-3,875	5,590	12,785	9,573	23,565	2,510	2,142	-3,272	8,001	17,885	20,841	30,572	47,180	110,281	8,868	364,932

* These estimates are, in general, the "b" values (the slopes) of least-squares trend lines fitted to the 1947–54 time series of annual employments in each of the twenty industry groups for each of the forty-eight states. Since no data are available for 1948, we estimated all figures for that year by a straight line interpolation between the figures for the surrounding years, 1947 and 1949. Often data for other years would also be missing, particularly for states in which the given industry was quantitatively insignificant, so we made further interpolations. While for the more important industrial states, (roughly, from Massachusetts west to Illinois), a complete time series (1947, 1949–54) was available for almost every major industry group, for the Mountain and, to a lesser extent, Plains states, usually we could make only the roughest estimates of the various industrial trends because of spotty data.

In the not infrequent case of no data at all, or data for only one year, we estimated the average annual change in employment to be zero. The justification for this practice is that, usually, the lack of data was due to the quantitative insignificance of the industry in that state and, therefore, such employment change as did occur was probably of very small magnitude, rendering zero a fairly good approximation in most cases. Ordinarily, estimating practices were quite routine but one fairly frequent practice probably deserves mention. The year 1954, a time of national recession, was frequently a year of lesser employment than was the year 1947, even for industries which were decidedly not secularly declining industries. Therefore, in states for which data was available only for the years 1947 and 1954 (Census years), a trend based on those two years alone would have had a downward bias in most cases. And so, for those states, we estimated industry employments for 1953 by projecting the 1954 figures backward, using the national rate of change between those two years, that is, we adopted a figure which gave the state the same share of national employment in 1953 as it had in 1954. Next, we took an average of the 1953 and 1954 figures; we then positioned this figure between the two years and a straight-line trend was fitted to that figure from the 1947 origin year.

The saving grace of all of this is that the time series are always most complete for those states which are the more important centers of a given industry and, fortunately, it is those same states which have the strongest influence on the correlation coefficients, which latter are, of course, the ends for which the various industry trends were derived.

Derived from Department of Commerce, Bureau of the Census, Census of Manufactures: 1947, Census of Manufactures: 1954 and Annual Survey of Manufactures, for the years 1949–1953.

a Excluding industry group #202 which was not included in major industry group #20 until 1954.

b The time period used was 1949–54 because data for the year 1947 could not be made comparable with that for the remainder of the period.

Table A-2. Estimated Annual Rate of Change in Total Employment in Manufacturing Industries, by States, 1947-1954*

Major industry group

States	Food Y'_{20}	Tobacco Y'_{21}	Textiles Y'_{22}	Apparel Y'_{23}	Lumber Y'_{24}	Furniture Y'_{25}	Paper Y'_{26}	Printing Y'_{27}	Chemicals Y'_{28}	Petroleum & coal Y'_{29}	Rubber Y'_{30}	Leather Y'_{31}	Stone, clay & glass Y'_{32}	Primary metal Y'_{33}	Fabricated metal Y'_{34}	Machinery Y'_{35}	Electrical machinery Y'_{36}	Transportation equipment Y'_{37}	Instruments Y'_{38}	All manufacturing Y'_{40}
Maine	1.0243		.9516	.9792	1.0456	1.0201	1.0145	1.0021	.9752			1.0406	1.0258	.9553	1.0243	.9158		1.0204		1.0101
New Hampshire	1.0000		.9723	.8767	.9719	1.0543	1.0133	1.0373	.9537			1.0048	1.0696	.9984	1.0377	1.0222			1.1952a	1.0154
Vermont	.9989		.9182	1.0594	.9725	.9648	.9522	1.0318	.9447			1.0250	1.0686	.9952	1.0181	1.0615				1.0187
Massachusetts	.9782	.9890	.9292	1.0240	.9739	1.0201	1.0053	1.0015	.9872	.9878	1.0097	.9960	1.0090	1.0120	1.0012	1.0002	1.0743	1.0367	1.0220	1.0018
Rhode Island	.9877		.9621	1.0468	.9980	.9586	.9808	1.0135	.9978		.9907	1.0845	1.0980	1.0359	1.0078	.9919	.9936		1.0520	.9941
Connecticut	1.0024		.9586	1.0127	1.0210	1.0244	1.0145	1.0242	1.0373	1.0740a	1.0360	1.0700	.9867	.9835	.9869	1.0189	1.0244	1.1392	.9991	1.0223
New York	.9952	.9188	.9538	.9981	1.0054	1.0031	1.0089	1.0001	1.0047	.9610	1.0241	.9860	1.0067	1.0193	1.0233	1.0275	1.0505	1.0816	1.0097	1.0170
New Jersey	1.0215	.9618	.9587	1.0166	1.0236	1.0282	1.0243	1.0336	1.0045	1.0135	.9884	1.0092	1.0294	1.0053	1.0303	1.0223	1.0386	1.0566	1.0615	1.0194
Pennsylvania	.9851	.9771	.9579	1.0049	.9879	1.0490	1.0143	1.0120	1.0195	.9967	1.0100	.9914	.9937	1.0115	1.0071	1.0092	1.0415	1.0296	1.0525	1.0092
Ohio	.9944	.9028	1.0337	.9850	.9983	.9813	1.0126	1.0261	1.0271	1.0245	.9942	.9592	1.0154	1.0163	1.0117	1.0124	1.0169	1.1060	1.0213	1.0237
Indiana	.9839	.9399	.8921	.9833	1.0322	1.0018	1.0102	1.0150	1.0557	.967	.9990	.9663	1.0270	1.0200	1.0151	.9997	1.0604	1.0532	1.0097	1.0267
Illinois	.9876	.9497	.9893	.9752	1.0153	1.0033	1.0172	.9926	1.0122	1.0070	1.0283	.9596	1.0140	1.0099	1.0168	1.0044	1.0348	1.0422	1.0184	1.0105
Michigan	.9959	.9545	.9282	1.0207	.9605	1.0028	1.0235	1.0213	1.0221	1.0340	.9785	.9895	1.0245	.9945	1.0226	1.0374	1.0029	1.0152	1.0922	1.0192
Wisconsin	.9911		.9428	.9914	1.0223	.9884	1.0247	1.0244	1.0881	1.0211	.9803	.9761	°	1.0212	.9958	1.0041	1.0522	1.0153	1.0248	1.0167
Minnesota	.9847		.9349	1.0050	1.0009	.9978	1.0442	1.0080	1.0121	1.0124	1.0090	.9906	1.0370	.9678	1.0050	1.0165	.9062	1.1130	1.1413	1.0243
Iowa	1.0164			.9843	1.0421	1.0245	1.0824	1.0254	1.0363	1.0512	1.0548	.9640	1.0238	1.0890	1.0412	1.0448	1.0934	1.0776		1.0273
Missouri	.9800		1.0220	.9939	.9681	.9847	1.0216	1.0114	1.0254			.9811	1.0010	1.0128	1.0262	1.0183	1.0449	1.1110	1.0392	1.0273
North Dakota	.9240				.9751			1.0330					1.0573		1.0596	1.1862				1.0338
South Dakota	1.0099				1.1349b	1.0130	°	1.0301	.8934				1.0190	°	1.2273	.9328				1.0123
Nebraska	.9982			1.0322		°	1.0072	1.0226	1.0219			.9926	1.0510	°	1.1025	1.0400	1.0127	.9494		1.0347
Kansas	.9611			1.0179	1.0415	.9495		1.0456	1.1201	1.0045			1.0600	.9444	1.0700	1.1012		1.3036		1.1033
Delaware	1.0076		.9911	1.0450	.9469	°	1.0036	1.0600	.9993	.9852		.9475	1.1144	1.0142	.9425	1.0091		1.1540		1.0306
Maryland	1.0058		.9359	1.0168	1.0272	1.0775	1.0338	1.0200	.9794	1.0368	1.0228	.9720	1.0125	1.0127	1.0087	1.0270	1.0747	1.0657	1.0100	1.0262
District of Columbia	.9665			.9958		1.0161	1.0346	1.0105	1.0353				1.0223		1.0144	1.1182	1.0806a			1.0194
Virginia	1.0190	.9833	1.0223	1.0515	.9576	1.0130	1.0114	1.0444	1.0242		1.0846a	.9951	1.0588	.9811	1.0523	1.0666		1.0434	1.0480	1.0228

State	(1)	(2)	(3)	(4)	(5)	(6)	(7)	(8)	(9)	(10)	(11)	(12)	(13)	(14)	(15)	(16)	(17)	(18)	(19)	(20)
West Virginia	.9910	1.0177	.9516	1.0222	.9890	1.0328	1.0087	1.0043	1.0170	1.0259		.9084	.9706	1.0084	.9849	1.0347	1.0338		1.2180^a	1.0010
North Carolina	.9664	1.0151		1.0382	.9542	1.0343	1.0300	1.0518	1.0293	1.0264		.9798	1.0272	1.0175	1.0890	1.0921		.9717		1.0242
South Carolina	.9660	1.0103		1.0035	.9874	1.0040	1.0017	1.0500	1.2839			.9603	°	1.2765^b	1.0465	1.1222		.8957^a	1.5328^a	1.0259
Georgia	1.0315	1.0073		1.0547	.9328	1.0478	1.0852	1.0375	.9951	1.0230	1.0090	1.0152	1.0078	1.0755	1.0145	1.0968	1.3171			1.0282
Florida	1.0460	1.0035	1.2636^a	1.1750	.9342	1.1377	1.1065	1.0629	1.1192	1.3790^a	1.1981^a	1.1117	1.1597^b	1.1817	1.1013	1.2338^a	1.0177			1.0714
Kentucky	.9920	1.0205	1.0124	1.0370	.9642	.9677	1.0200	1.0672	1.0289	1.0273		.9562	1.0173	.9945	1.0143	1.0511	1.0290	1.0705	.9783	1.0254
Tennessee	.9982	.9932		1.0619	.9808	1.0401	1.0706	1.0157	1.0740	.9646	.9837	.9957	1.0045	.9714	1.0236	1.0810	1.0073	1.0387	1.0438	1.0335
Alabama	1.0116	.9888	1.1317	.9612	1.0419	1.0722	1.0246	.9908	1.0277			1.0231	1.0063	1.0454	.9751	1.0621				1.0144
Mississippi	1.0020	.9987	1.0849	.9979	1.1259	1.0942	1.0306	1.0250	1.0277	1.0200		1.0284	.9293^b	1.2640^b	1.0804					1.0331
Arkansas	1.0392		1.0887	.9800	1.0752	1.0329	1.0288	1.0542	1.0264		1.1484	1.0142	.9637	1.1541	.9704		1.0705			1.0360
Louisiana	.9980	1.0017	1.0022	.9865	1.0080	1.0263	1.0227	1.0450	1.0178		1.0481	1.2765^b	1.0222	1.0928	.9984	1.0775				1.0232
Oklahoma	.9731		1.1668	.9741	1.0488	1.0609	1.0188	°	.9990		1.4544^a	1.0568	1.0371	1.0863	1.0833	1.3785	1.0227			1.0587
Texas	.9981	1.0088	1.0448	.9372	1.0797	1.0776	1.0317	1.0757	1.0150		1.1263	1.0318	1.1176	1.0388	1.0572	1.1528	1.1721	1.1617		1.0513
Montana	.9870			1.0727	1.0253	1.1077					.9794	.9944	.9594	1.0484	.9704	.9837?	1.0679			1.1470
Idaho	1.0101			1.0555	.9968	1.2996					.9630	1.0402	2317	9562	0928		1.2238^a			1.0589
Wyoming	.9659		1.0087	1.0317							.0252									1.0125
Colorado	.9939	1.0245	1.0376	1.0454	1.0214	1.0352	1.1481	1.0353	1.0322		1.1383	1.0212	1.0082	1.0420	1.0326	1.1877^a	1.0304		1.1034	1.0258
New Mexico	1.0324	.9931	1.0087	.9696	1.0522	1.0253	1.0264			1.1386^b	°	1.0410	°	1.0704	1.0928	1.0705	1.1260
Arizona	1.0018	1.4378^b	1.0062	1.0432	1.5232^b	.9968	1.0178		1.0260	1.0390	1.1391	1.2233^b	.9984	1.6961^a	1.0958
Utah	.9950	1.0405	.9921	.9973	1.1260	.2996	.9990		1.0420	1.0386	1.1265	1.1128	1.3785	1.6178^a	1.0418
Nevada	.9420		1.0471	1.0646	1.0928	1.0317	1.0447		1.1836						1.1222
Washington	.9774	1.0118	1.0493	1.0124	.9860	1.0315	1.0083	1.2438	1.0048		1.0403	.9256^a	1.0122	.9091	1.0759	.0387	1.0656	.0278	1.1132	1.0490
Oregon	.9850	.9836	1.0425	1.0483	.9380	1.0462	1.0116	1.0524	1.0199		1.1319^a	.9256^a	1.0091	1.0128	1.0581	.9998	.9863	.0867	1.0405
California	1.0114	1.0222	1.0390	1.0555	1.0358	1.0862	1.0288	1.0303	.9983		1.0118	1.0341	1.0470	1.0607	1.0541	1.2050	1.1574	1.1118	1.0761
United States	.9945	.9780	.9824	1.0130	.9931	1.0168	1.0262	1.0128	1.0340	1.0117	1.0080	.9912	1.0165	1.0148	1.0202	1.0186	1.0508	1.0748	1.0328	1.0238

* For the eight major industry groups which were manually processed (21, 22, 29, 30, 31, 36, 37 and 38), we simply eliminated annual rates of change which were inordinately high or low out of unusually small bases (e.g., a thousand workers or less) from the computation of the related correlation coefficients. For the twelve industry groups which were machine processed (20, 23, 24, 25, 26, 27, 28, 32, 33, 34, 35 and 40) the data had to be drawn from a common set of states. By eliminating six states (N.D., S.D., Mont., Ida., Wyo. and Nev.) and the District of Columbia we formed a sub-set of forty-two states which could be made common to all twelve of the industry groups—with minor modifications of the data. Specifically, we could not simply eliminate inordinately high and low rates of change because the data-processing program would not tolerate non-entries; instead, we normalized inadmissible rates of change by substituting the national rate of change for that industry for the unusual state rate. And, to avoid gaps in the data, we imputed the national rate of change for a given industry to a state if no data had been reported for that state—we hypothecated the data.

^{a} Figure deleted.
^{b} Figure normalized by substituting the national rate of change.
^{c} Figure hypothecated by imputing the national rate of change.

APPENDIX B

INDEPENDENT VARIABLES: INDUSTRY-GENERAL FORMS

TABLE B-1

Symbol	Description
X_1	Average annual change in total population, 1940–1947 (in thousands)
X_2	Average annual change in personal income, 1940–1947 (in tens of millions of dollars)
X_3	Average annual change in personal income, 1945–1948 (in tens of millions of dollars)
X_4	Average annual change in total manufacturing employment 1939–1947 (in thousands)
X_5	Expenditures for new plant and equipment, 1947 (in millions of dollars)
X_6	Average annual number of patents and designs issued to citizens, 1946–1948 (in tens)
X_7	State and local taxes as a per cent of state personal income, 1953
X_8	Estimated state and local taxes paid by business per non-agricultural employee, 1953 (in dollars)[a]
X_9	Average hourly earnings in manufacturing industries 1949[b]
X_{10}	Estimated trade union membership as a percent of non-agricultural employment, 1947
X_{11}	Median years of school completed by persons twenty-five years old and over, 1950
X_{12}	Number of persons twenty-five years old and over who have completed four or more years of college, 1950 (in thousands)
X_{13}	Total staff, institutions of higher education, 1947–1948 (in hundreds)

[a] The estimates of the amounts of state and local taxes paid by business in each of the states were prepared by Professor Harvey E. Brazer of the University of Michigan. These estimates were fashioned as follows:

...our estimate is of total taxes *paid by business*, other than severance taxes, other taxes on specially designated business such as public utilities, banks, and so forth. Of course where the latter pay general taxes the amounts involved are not separable. We have not included sales taxes, general or selective, not on the ground that these are shifted (the other taxes are probably shifted in varying degrees, too), but because the payment of the tax is not determined by the state or community in which the *plant* is located. In other words, to the extent possible, we have concentrated on those taxes that may influence plant location decisions in manufacturing.

Except for the local property tax, the taxes paid by business are simply state totals of collections. In the case of the property tax we allocated the total to business according to the ratio of assessed value of industrial and commercial plus personal property (other than motor vehicles) to total assessed value of locally assessed property in the state. The source of data for the latter computation is U. S. Department of Commerce, Bureau of the Census, *Property Tax Assessments in the United States, 1957*, "Census of Governments Advance Releases," No. 5 (Washington, 1957), but this is all we have. (Quoted from a letter from Professor Brazer, dated January 16, 1958.)

[b] We derived the annual figures in the table by averaging the data reported by the BLS for the months January, April, July and October of a given year. The data used here apply to the year 1949 for 37 states but we have estimated the figures for

Table B-1. General Variables Associated with Average Annual Change in Total Employment in Manufacturing Industries, by States, 1947–1954*

States	X_1	X_2	X_3	X_4	X_5	X_6	X_7	X_8	X_9	X_{10}	X_{11}	X_{12}	X_{13}
Me.	.7	8	7	2.2	35	5	8.9	91	1.15	15.3	10.2	25	10
N.H.	2.4	5	5	1.7	24	5	8.1	94	1.19	17.2	9.8	19	10
Vt.	−1.3	3	3	1.4	10	3	9.4	116	1.16	15.7	10.0	13	8
Mass.	38.7	46	42	21.1	199	116	8.5	137	1.34	23.8	10.9	208	105
R.I.	9.3	8	4	3.0	35	36	6.8	95	1.24	20.0	9.3	28	12
Conn.	37.3	25	24	14.8	116	76	5.8	76	1.38	20.0	9.8	87	35
N.Y.	76.7	175	182	70.6	497	424	8.6	119	1.50	29.5	9.6	695	276
N.J.	64.7	55	44	25.9	304	223	6.4	116	1.47	27.0	9.3	206	43
Pa.	43.6	105	108	53.0	534	171	6.0	88	1.33	34.6	9.0	340	148
Ohio	110.9	90	97	57.9	498	185	5.6	69	1.51	32.2	9.9	271	106
Ind.	49.4	43	44	26.3	302	58	6.8	90	1.48	32.2	9.6	120	62
Ill.	62.7	110	143	54.0	478	228	6.2	69	1.48	33.8	9.3	318	140
Mich.	108.6	75	79	44.4	428	121	6.9	100	1.62	33.3	9.9	194	67
Wis.	15.3	35	38	20.6	163	54	8.8	152	1.38	34.4	8.9	108	55
Minn.	.9	29	41	9.7	83	30	9.1	141	1.36	32.4	9.0	97	56
Iowa	−4.0	24	49	6.5	65	16	9.4	94	1.37	21.7	9.8	78	50
Mo.	8.6	39	45	13.4	132	39	6.0	52	1.32	32.1	8.8	119	65
N.D.	−8.9	9	8	.1	2	2	11.2	13	1.19	13.6	8.7	15	8
S.D.	−5.9	7	10	.4	3	1	10.4	155	1.20	11.3	8.9	18	10
Neb.	−7.1	14	15	2.6	18	4	7.8	78	1.20	16.6	10.1	39	24
Kan.	9.0	23	14	4.0	37	11	8.9	95	1.36	19.4	10.2	67	42
Del.	5.3	3	4	1.4	21	25	4.0	61	1.24	13.9	9.8	14	5
Md.	59.6	25	16	7.8	124	32	6.1	59	1.44	19.5	8.9	95	43
D.C.	26.1	10	6	.4	5	19	5.9	45	1.40	21.5	12.0	68	33
Va.	79.0	29	6	8.3	112	17	6.0	67	1.11	15.4	8.5	113	39
W.Va.	−3.6	17	22	5.0	82	9	6.8	29	1.40	43.1	8.5	45	16
N.C.	28.3	31	24	11.0	138	9	8.2	90	1.07	6.5	7.9	102	50
S.C.	13.4	14	11	6.6	62	3	8.5	79	1.04	7.0	7.6	54	23
Ga.	21.7	26	12	9.1	84	8	7.6	57	1.00	11.6	7.8	79	39
Fla.	89.1	27	5	2.0	50	15	8.8	67	.98	14.1	9.6	103	28
Ky.	−8.1	21	22	6.6	77	8	6.4	55	1.31	23.9	8.4	59	28
Tenn.	33.3	25	14	8.7	84	11	7.1	61	1.11	19.5	8.4	72	47
Ala.	14.1	22	13	9.6	72	7	6.9	34	1.10	21.1	7.9	57	30
Miss.	−9.7	13	9	3.1	23	2	9.3	84	.90	11.2	8.1	41	22
Ark.	−17.1	12	9	3.0	30	4	7.9	81	.94	17.7	8.3	31	20
La.	29.9	20	15	5.6	97	11	10.2	61	1.20	15.3	7.6	67	38
Okla.	−27.4	19	13	2.2	26	20	8.9	83	1.29	13.7	9.1	77	32
Tex.	137.0	79	63	16.6	305	43	6.6	67	1.28	14.0	9.3	254	102
Mont.	−4.0	6	10	.5	7	3	7.5	141	1.53	42.6	10.1	20	9
Ida.	0.0	6	5	.6	11	2	9.2	133	1.51	18.2	10.6	17	8
Wyo.	.9	3	4	.2	10	1	8.7	140	1.66	27.8	11.1	11	4
Colo.	15.1	15	15	2.7	32	12	8.9	113	1.35	23.4	10.9	62	22
N.M.	7.3	5	5	.4	5	3	8.5	43	1.30	12.9	9.3	22	9
Ariz.	21.9	7	7	.8	8	3	8.4	86	1.40	22.9	10.0	29	7
Utah	12.0	7	4	1.1	17	3	8.3	81	1.39	23.3	12.0	26	14
Nev.	5.1	2	1	.2	3	1	7.6	100	1.64	25.2	11.5	7	2
Wash.	69.3	31	14	5.6	81	21	7.9	56	1.64	48.2	11.2	102	32
Ore.	39.7	20	17	4.8	62	11	8.2	24	1.67	37.5	10.9	61	23
Calif.	423.1	154	81	38.4	411	200	8.2	136	1.60	30.4	11.6	533	171

* *The somewhat unusual units in which the data are reported (scaling) are attributable to the fact that the programming of the correlation process (for a high-speed, electronic computer) was facilitated by restricting the data to three significant digits.*

the remainder from later data. The figures for six states (Ida., La., Mass., Neb., Nev., and N. D.) are those reported for the year 1950 and adjusted backward to 1949 by using the national rate of change in average hourly earnings between those two years, that is, by assuming that these states stood in the same relative position to the national average in 1949 as they did in 1950. And we adjusted the data for four states (Colo., Ky., Mont., and W. Va.) backward from 1951. Finally, we drew data for Ohio largely from the year 1952. As no figures were reported for the District of Columbia, we used the national average hourly earnings, not because they are likely to apply, but because the statistical process employed requires a value for each areal unit and this is no more arbitrary than any alternative value which we might have selected.

Sources:

X_1:   Department of Commerce, Office of Business Economics, *Personal Income by States* (Washington, 1956), Table 3, pp. 144–5.

X_2:   *Ibid.*, Table 1, pp. 140–1.

X_3:   *Ibid.*

X_4:   Department of Commerce, Bureau of the Census, *Census of Manufactures: 1947.*

X_5:   *Ibid.*

X_6:   Bureau of the Census, *Statistical Abstract of the United States: 1954.* (75th ed., Washington, 1954), Table 588, p. 521.

X_7:   Department of Commerce, Bureau of the Census, *State and Local Government Revenue in 1953*, Special Study No. 37 (Washington, 1955), Table 2, and *Compendium of State Government Finances in 1953* (Washington, 1954), Tables 5–7.

X_8:   *Ibid.* and *Property Tax Assessments in the United States, 1957*, "Census of Governments Advance Releases," No. 5 (Washington, 1957), pp. 12–13.

X_9:   Department of Labor, Bureau of Labor Statistics, *Monthly Labor Review*, February 1950, Table C-5, p. 237 and supplementary data in various issues through March 1951.

X_{10}:   National Bureau of Economic Research, *Basic Research and the Analysis of Business Conditions, Thirty-sixth Annual Report* (New York, May 1956), Table 7, p. 46.

X_{11}:   Department of Commerce, Bureau of the Census, *U. S. Census of Population: 1950*, Vol. II, Part 1.

X_{12}:   *Ibid.*

X_{13}:   Federal Security Agency, Office of Education, *Biennial Survey of Education in the United States—1946–48*, Chapter 4, "Statistics of Higher Education, 1947–48" (Washington, 1950), Table 5, pp. 66–67.

TABLE B-2

Symbol	Description
X_1'	Annual rate of change in state population, 1940–47.
X_2'	Annual rate of change in state personal income, 1940–47.
X_3'	Annual rate of change in state personal income, 1945–48.
X_4'	Annual rate of change in total manufacturing employment, 1939–47.
X_5'	Expenditures for new plant and equipment in all manufacturing industries per manufacturing employee, 1947.
X_6'	Average annual number of patents and designs issued to residents per 100,000 residents, 1946–48.
X_{12}'	Percent of persons twenty-five years old and over who have completed four or more years of college, 1950.
X_{13}'	Total staff at institutions of higher education (1947–48) as a percent of persons twenty-five years old and over (1950).

Table B-2. General Variables Associated with Rate of Change in Total Employment in Manufacturing Industries, by States, 1947–1954

States	X_1'	X_2'	X_3'	X_4'	X_5'	X_6'	X_{12}'	X_{13}'
Me.	1.0009	1.1200	1.0802	1.0251	350	5.9	4.83	1.86
N.H.	1.0049	1.1162	1.0876	1.0254	321	9.9	5.97	3.00
Vt.	.9964	1.1129	1.0960	1.0474	278	7.9	5.88	3.99
Mass.	1.0088	1.0997	1.0669	1.0340	277	25.3	7.19	3.61
R.I.	1.0124	1.1125	1.0373	1.0228	236	47.5	5.77	2.50
Conn.	1.0208	1.1140	1.0808	1.0450	291	39.2	6.98	2.77
N.Y.	1.0056	1.1079	1.0815	1.0490	280	30.2	7.36	2.92
N.J.	1.0148	1.1130	1.0630	1.0420	412	49.5	6.76	1.40
Pa.	1.0044	1.1151	1.0860	1.0445	371	17.1	5.41	2.35
Ohio	1.0153	1.1307	1.0945	1.0632	417	23.8	5.71	2.24
Ind.	1.0138	1.1460	1.0933	1.0624	551	15.5	5.22	2.71
Ill.	1.0078	1.1256	1.1141	1.0586	404	27.5	5.91	2.60
Mich.	1.0193	1.1364	1.0991	1.0583	439	19.9	5.29	1.83
Wis.	1.0048	1.1343	1.0979	1.0650	391	16.7	5.37	2.74
Minn.	1.0003	1.1328	1.1305	1.0733	460	10.6	5.64	3.25
Iowa	.9984	1.1296	1.1694	1.0600	461	6.4	5.04	3.23
Mo.	1.0022	1.1310	1.1012	1.0508	404	10.2	4.97	2.71
N.D.	.9856	1.2070	1.1347	1.0302	431	4.0	4.47	2.60
S.D.	.9906	1.1815	1.1396	1.0440	328	2.5	4.92	2.74
Neb.	.9945	1.1538	1.0958	1.0758	391	3.3	5.10	3.10
Kan.	1.0050	1.1770	1.0663	1.0726	493	6.1	5.96	3.78
Del.	1.0186	1.0920	1.0844	1.0498	613	81.9	7.30	2.41
Md.	1.0296	1.1282	1.0536	1.0407	541	13.9	7.00	3.18
D.C.	1.0341	1.0953	1.0420	1.0269	253	20.4	12.98	6.26
Va.	1.0268	1.1455	1.0184	1.0469	519	5.3	6.28	2.14
W.Va.	.9981	1.1393	1.1273	1.0478	646	4.7	4.30	1.51
N.C.	1.0077	1.1631	1.0777	1.0334	361	2.4	5.03	2.49
S.C.	1.0070	1.1500	1.0712	1.0416	327	1.7	5.39	2.27
Ga.	1.0068	1.1540	1.0423	1.0441	337	2.6	4.46	2.18
Fla.	1.0411	1.1675	1.0179	1.0290	636	5.8	6.28	1.71
Ky.	.9971	1.1467	1.0957	1.0680	596	2.8	3.80	1.77
Tenn.	1.0110	1.1576	1.0506	1.0480	378	3.6	4.08	2.68
Ala.	1.0049	1.1653	1.0557	1.0600	351	2.3	3.64	1.90
Miss.	.9955	1.1668	1.0625	1.0496	296	1.1	3.85	2.10
Ark.	.9910	1.1484	1.0673	1.0592	463	1.9	3.12	2.00
La.	1.0121	1.1487	1.0650	1.0528	734	4.3	4.70	2.71
Okla.	.9878	1.1398	1.0641	1.0496	460	9.1	6.20	1.45
Tex.	1.0201	1.1700	1.0809	1.0771	1027	5.9	6.04	2.43
Mont.	.9927	1.1351	1.1505	1.0385	463	5.0	6.10	2.55
Ida.	1.0000	1.1524	1.0894	1.0470	677	4.6	5.45	2.56
Wyo.	1.0034	1.1403	1.1144	1.0307	2022	5.4	7.14	2.81
Colo.	1.0122	1.1513	1.1015	1.0670	595	9.6	8.14	2.85
N.M.	1.0132	1.1637	1.0974	1.0802	716	5.9	6.86	2.63
Ariz.	1.0390	1.1710	1.0943	1.0744	587	4.7	7.39	1.72
Utah	1.0205	1.1575	1.0580	1.0589	693	4.1	7.63	4.04
Nev.	1.0403	1.1467	1.0542	1.0762	1109	8.5	7.34	2.34
Wash.	1.0358	1.1638	1.0420	1.0481	565	9.0	7.19	2.29
Ore.	1.0331	1.1732	1.0912	1.0581	584	7.7	6.65	2.54
Calif.	1.0520	1.1614	1.0503	1.0806	618	19.6	8.12	2.60

APPENDIX C

INDEPENDENT VARIABLES: INDUSTRY-SPECIFIC FORMS

TABLE C-1

Symbol	Patent classes	Associated with the major industry group
X_{14}	23. Chemistry 260. Chemistry, carbon compounds 204. Chemistry, electrical & wave energy 71. Chemistry, fertilizers 18. Plastics	Chemicals & allied products (Y_{28})
X_{15}	49. Glass 215. Bottles & jars 25. Plastic block & earthenware apparatus 51. Abrading	Stone, clay & glass products (Y_{32})
X_{16}	75. Metallurgy 266. Metallurgical apparatus 148. Metal treatment 80. Metal rolling 205. Metal drawing 22. Metal founding	Primary metal industries (Y_{33})
X_{17}*	29. Metal working	Fabricated metal products (Y_{34})
X_{18}*	82. Turning 90. Gear cutting, milling & planning	Machinery, excluding electrical (Y_{35})
X_{19}*	123. Internal combustion engines	Transportation equipment (Y_{37})
X_{20}	88. Optics 95. Photography 33. Geometrical instruments 161. Time controlling mechanisms 128. Surgery 32. Dentistry 3. Artificial body members	Instruments & related products (Y_{38})

* *Average number for the two years, 1947–48.*

Table C-1. Number of Patents Granted to Residents, by States, 1947, in Selected Patent Classes Associated with Various Manufacturing Industries

States	X_{14}*	X_{15}	X_{16}	X_{17}	X_{18}	X_{19}	X_{20}
Me.	0	0	0	0	1	0	0
N.H.	4	1	1	1	1	0	3
Vt.	0	2	0	3	4	0	2
Mass.	83	36	14	15	5	12	59
R.I.	3	4	1	3	2	1	1
Conn.	118	11	22	15	10	47	18
N.Y.	286	53	55	34	20	27	218
N.J.	344	21	52	28	5	26	56
Pa.	185	31	67	30	8	14	44
Ohio	168	32	54	46	35	30	37
Ind.	51	16	11	8	1	35	16
Ill.	180	29	35	26	22	13	72
Mich.	68	29	35	44	17	80	28
Wis.	26	12	7	11	15	10	8
Minn.	3	9	4	4	0	7	10
Iowa	0	2	0	0	2	4	4
Mo.	41	4	4	2	1	11	5
N.D.	0	0	0	1	0	0	0
S.D.	0	1	0	0	0	0	0
Neb.	0	1	0	0	0	1	2
Kan.	0	0	1	3	0	1	2
Del.	135	0	3	1	0	2	6
Md.	35	11	17	10	2	3	10
D.C.	15	1	3	2	0	1	6
Va.	11	3	1	1	1	4	7
W.Va.	30	2	1	2	0	0	1
N.C.	4	4	1	0	0	1	5
S.C.	4	0	0	0	0	1	0
Ga.	11	1	0	1	1	1	2
Fla.	26	3	0	1	0	6	8
Ky.	6	0	3	1	1	0	3
Tenn.	7	2	1	1	0	0	3
Ala.	8	1	1	1	0	0	1
Miss.	2	0	0	0	0	2	1
Ark.	2	2	2	0	0	0	0
La.	22	2	2	1	1	1	1
Okla.	101	0	0	1	0	3	2
Tex.	31	10	2	4	2	4	11
Mont.	0	0	0	0	0	0	2
Ida.	0	0	0	0	0	0	1
Wyo.	1	1	1	0	0	0	1
Colo.	3	1	1	1	0	0	3
N.M.	0	1	1	0	0	0	1
Ariz.	0	0	2	0	0	2	2
Utah	3	0	3	0	0	1	0
Nev.	1	0	3	0	0	0	0
Wash.	6	3	3	3	2	2	7
Ore.	5	1	1	1	0	1	9
Calif.	146	26	29	25	15	31	77
U.S. total	2,175	369	444	331	174	385	755

* Patent grants in Class No. 260 were so numerous that we drew a sample consisting of the grants made in the first week of each month of 1947 and these twelve-week state totals were multiplied by 52/12 to derive an estimate of the annual state totals for that patent class.
Source: Department of Commerce, Official Gazette of the United States Patent Office, 1947–48.

Table C-2. Expenditures for New Plant and Equipment in Manufacturing Industries, by States, 1947, in Dollars*

Major industry groups

States	Food X_{21} (10⁵)	Tobacco X_{22} (10⁵)	Textiles X_{23} (10⁵)	Apparel X_{24} (10⁵)	Lumber X_{25} (10⁵)	Furniture X_{26} (10⁴)	Paper X_{27} (10⁵)	Printing X_{28} (10⁵)	Chemicals X_{29} (10⁵)	Petroleum & coal X_{30} (10⁵)	Rubber X_{31} (10⁵)	Leather X_{32} (10⁴)	Stone, clay & glass X_{33} (10⁵)	Primary Metal X_{34} (10⁵)	Fabricated Metal X_{35} (10⁵)	Machinery X_{36} (10⁵)	Electrical Machinery X_{37} (10⁵)	Transportation Equipment X_{38} (10⁵)	Instruments X_{39} (10⁵)	All Manufacturing X_{40} (10⁶)
Me.	43	0	69	2	26	18	151	5	0	0	0	132	2	0	0	25	0	0	0	35
N. H.	13	0	75	6	10	21	70	7	0	0	0	122	8	0	3	11	0	0	0	24
Vt.	16	0	11	1	13	38	7	1	0	0	0	7	10	0	7	15	0	0	0	10
Mass.	167	0	331	47	17	168	175	69	18	16	84	670	62	6	99	210	178	9	27	199
R. I.	27	0	131	6	1	13	0	7	1	0	16	5	3	1	16	38	13	0	2	35
Conn.	52	0	116	13	3	40	41	37	7	0	52	12	26	11	162	213	82	5	28	116
N. Y.	751	3	207	209	30	688	361	370	66	111	52	416	231	33	221	407	322	14	275	497
N. J.	272	8	208	49	8	147	147	50	94	166	51	113	119	17	127	169	299	8	46	304
Pa.	493	14	438	95	30	356	256	326	42	451	111	260	347	106	286	420	289	13	40	534
Ohio	373	2	35	31	16	595	270	216	49	275	302	179	236	82	421	762	201	39	18	498
Ind.	255	0	11	9	18	420	68	38	24	689	80	10	130	61	134	323	110	23	5	302
Ill.	748	0	20	38	28	948	210	266	45	210	0	150	163	52	383	847	436	16	55	479
Mich.	300	1	12	8	45	407	218	48	56	30	67	74	89	46	305	403	58	159	7	428
Wis.	445	0	30	10	36	355	303	58	4	3	0	305	0	6	100	229	62	12	10	163
Minn.	245	0	8	17	18	72	106	40	6	15	0	10	17	2	43	72	106	1	0	83
Iowa	204	0	0	4	10	31	4	34	6	0	20	7	40	1	21	200	11	1	2	65
Mo.	378	0	6	33	11	162	32	50	18	0	0	184	70	8	109	47	61	6	3	132
N. D.	17	0	0	0	0	0	0	1	0	0	0	0	2	0	1	1	0	0	0	2
S. D.	25	0	0	0	2	0	0	1	0	0	0	0	3	0	1	1	0	0	0	3
Neb.	97	0	0	3	1	36	0	23	1	1	0	1	5	0	5	8	5	0	0	18
Kan.	92	0	0	1	2	15	11	8	5	64	0	2	67	0	20	20	0	2	0	37
Del.	24	0	26	12	0	0	6	2	9	0	0	33	1	0	8	8	0	0	0	21
Md.	129	0	17	16	13	43	49	21	15	58	18	38	101	48	65	57	19	2	1	124

98

State	1	2	3	4	5	6	7	8	9	10	11	12	13	14	15	16	17	18	19	20
D. C.	20	0	0	0	0	0	3	17	0	0	0	0	1	0	2	0	0	0	0	5
Va.	95	56	210	13	33	439	79	15	41	1	0	41	88	1	10	3	0	3	0	112
W. Va.	40	0	13	1	12	28	7	6	34	0	0	13	90	13	25	12	13	0	0	82
N. C.	73	157	734	13	56	631	157	12	4	0	0	22	25	0	10	11	0	0	0	138
S. C.	35	0	394	13	42	67	64	4	2	0	0	1	20	0	1	0	0	0	0	62
Ga.	87	0	246	27	51	348	106	42	43	2	0	25	39	1	9	24	4	0	0	84
Fla.	152	12	0	3	27	37	170	31	5	0	0	0	25	0	13	3	1	0	0	50
Ky.	169	77	9	14	16	178	3	57	7	10	0	0	19	3	27	211	27	0	0	77
Tenn.	122	0	109	15	32	224	61	17	23	0	0	64	38	7	39	12	19	2	0	84
Ala.	60	0	121	26	57	46	42	7	4	22	0	0	38	29	15	18	0	0	0	72
Miss.	44	0	15	6	55	0	39	3	3	0	0	0	15	0	1	2	0	0	0	23
Ark.	57	0	0	2	61	76	36	7	6	17	0	35	28	1	4	1	0	0	0	30
La.	171	0	4	7	50	23	168	10	27	216	0	1	41	0	13	6	0	1	0	97
Okla.	57	0	0	1	4	32	0	12	1	79	0	0	44	1	9	19	0	0	0	26
Tex.	318	0	19	23	56	221	171	57	132	692	0	50	94	7	59	96	17	1	5	305
Mont.	33	0	0	0	25	0	0	2	0	5	0	0	2	0	0	0	0	0	0	7
Ida.	75	0	0	0	27	0	0	2	0	0	0	0	3	0	0	1	0	0	0	11
Wyo.	6	0	0	0	3	0	0	0	0	91	0	0	2	0	0	0	0	0	0	10
Colo.	87	0	0	1	10	15	0	16	2	47	0	9	40	5	5	15	0	0	1	32
N. M.	12	0	0	0	4	6	0	1	3	0	0	0	1	0	1	0	0	0	0	5
Ariz.	30	0	0	0	22	6	0	7	0	0	0	0	7	0	3	0	0	0	0	8
Utah	55	0	0	1	0	10	0	4	0	9	0	0	42	4	5	3	0	0	0	17
Nev.	5	0	0	0	0	0	0	0	1	0	0	0	0	0	0	0	0	0	0	3
Wash.	160	0	1	4	195	63	289	29	3	0	0	5	27	2	11	16	1	2	0	81
Ore.	116	0	9	1	298	59	59	48	2	0	0	9	18	1	7	6	4	0	0	62
Calif.	960	0	32	58	231	561	164	177	38	412	0	107	334	39	238	226	79	23	0	411
U. S.	8,208	356	3,675	839	1,716	7,744	4,068	2,264	811	3,998	1,098	3,130	2,851	592	3,048	5,176	2,446	355	560	6,004

99

* Figures are expressed in tens of thousands (10^4), hundreds of thousands (10^5) and millions (10^6) of dollars. Data were scaled to hold to a maximum of three significant figures.
Source: Department of Commerce, Bureau of the Census, Census of Manufactures 1947.

Table C-3. Employment in Manufacturing Industries, by States, 1947*

Major industry group

States	Food X_{41} (000)	Tobacco X_{42} (00)	Textiles X_{43} (000)	Apparel X_{44} (000)	Lumber X_{45} (00)	Furniture X_{46} (00)	Paper X_{47} (00)	Printing X_{48} (000)	Chemicals X_{49} (00)	Petroleum & coal X_{50} (00)	Rubber X_{51} (00)	Leather X_{52} (00)	Stone, clay & glass X_{53} (00)	Primary metals X_{54} (000)	Fabricated metals X_{55} (000)	Machinery X_{56} (000)	Electrical machinery X_{57} (000)	Transportation equipment X_{58} (000)	Instruments X_{59} (00)	All manufacturing X_{60} (0000)
Me.	8	0	26	4	123	7	165	2	7	0	2	157	6	0	2	6	0	3	0	10
N. H.	2	5	20	2	0	14	58	2	5	0	0	201	10	1	2	6	0	0	5	7
Vt.	2	0	5	2	0	18	27	1	3	0	0	5	26	1	1	7	0	0	0	3
Mass.	43	4	127	47	0	110	349	35	180	25	264	709	105	20	41	87	56	18	161	72
R. I.	4	0	62	3	0	8	20	3	13	0	67	4	11	5	8	17	5	0	17	15
Conn.	8	4	39	16	0	24	75	11	77	3	106	16	58	35	56	78	34	29	186	40
N. Y.	129	22	90	381	0	374	644	166	674	76	88	690	392	77	88	138	101	90	873	177
N. J.	46	53	63	71	0	75	214	20	822	162	169	102	283	39	43	66	94	44	177	74
Pa.	98	194	139	142	0	178	353	55	437	293	151	312	719	262	115	136	93	65	206	144
Ohio	61	27	11	31	95	243	317	50	372	110	828	178	600	177	123	227	91	94	93	119
Ind.	42	14	7	16	0	214	90	16	203	165	156	30	211	82	41	75	55	80	26	55
Ill.	132	8	12	60	128	292	281	91	475	171	53	288	307	101	115	218	130	46	312	119
Mich.	44	9	6	9	161	215	260	22	340	35	151	44	156	93	92	151	23	377	48	98
Wis.	43	0	11	10	158	125	281	17	59	11	56	213	0	24	36	94	29	30	59	42
Minn.	40	0	5	9	0	28	120	18	50	15	6	16	36	7	11	24	9	3	71	18
Iowa	44	0	0	4	0	22	13	9	52	0	23	8	46	3	5	35	5	3	9	14
Mo.	47	19	3	37	0	75	91	22	156	25	0	43	150	13	23	24	17	24	29	33
N. D.	3	0	0	0	0	0	0	1	0	0	0	0	2	0	0	0	0	0	0	1
S. D.	6	0	0	0	0	0	0	1	2	0	0	0	3	0	0	0	0	0	0	1
Neb.	24	0	0	1	0	10	0	4	15	2	0	0	10	0	1	3	2	2	0	5
Kan.	26	0	0	2	0	10	14	6	51	45	0	1	33	1	4	5	0	10	0	7
Del.	5	0	3	2	0	0	8	1	70	1	0	31	3	3	2	3	0	1	3	3

State	1	2	3	4	5	6	7	8	9	10	11	12	13	14	15	16	17	18	19	20
Md.	32	2	6	24	0	27	55	10	181	24	57	33	68	31	17	10	9	33	10	23
D. C.	4	0	0	0	0	2	7	0	2	0	0	0	3	0	0	0	0	0	2	2
Va.	20	167	34	15	233	139	107	6	338	3	7	53	45	4	6	2	0	17	12	22
W. Va.	6	11	4	4	0	9	16	3	206	24	1	18	303	22	11	3	5	0	1	13
N. C.	16	325	210	17	311	279	79	5	95	0	0	16	56	2	3	4	0	1	0	38
S. C.	7	20	125	11	0	25	58	2	36	0	0	0	31	1	0	1	0	1	0	19
Ga.	26	0	103	25	340	57	73	6	111	5	0	24	70	3	3	6	1	4	0	25
Fla.	19	87	0	2	0	20	57	6	47	0	0	2	27	0	2	1	0	5	0	8
Ky.	23	92	4	13	116	72	7	6	48	13	0	34	42	8	11	10	5	3	13	13
Tenn.	21	19	37	19	191	79	48	9	282	6	62	104	81	15	15	6	1	5	17	22
Ala.	11	0	52	8	374	16	57	4	82	28	47	0	63	39	7	7	0	8	0	21
Miss.	7	0	5	11	286	16	48	2	48	0	0	0	20	0	0	1	0	0	0	8
Ark.	9	0	0	2	282	32	32	2	41	12	0	13	25	3	1	0	0	0	10	7
La.	28	8	2	6	291	13	142	4	129	127	0	0	34	1	4	2	0	9	1	13
Okla.	13	0	0	1	0	12	4	5	16	75	12	0	44	3	4	6	0	1	5	6
Tex.	56	4	8	22	307	58	47	18	236	377	11	17	106	12	13	23	2	21	9	30
Mont.	4	0	0	0	0	1	0	1	4	6	0	0	6	4	0	0	0	0	0	2
Ida.	5	0	0	0	0	0	0	1	1	0	0	0	3	1	0	0	0	0	0	2
Wyo.	1	0	0	0	0	0	0	0	0	22	0	0	3	0	0	0	0	0	0	1
Colo.	15	0	0	2	0	7	6	5	13	8	0	12	24	8	2	4	0	1	4	5
N.M.	2	0	0	0	0	1	0	1	5	0	0	0	3	0	0	0	0	0	0	1
Ariz.	3	0	0	0	0	3	0	2	6	0	0	0	9	3	0	0	0	0	0	1
Utah	7	1	1	1	0	4	0	2	6	4	0	0	11	7	1	1	0	0	0	2
Nev.	1	0	0	0	0	0	0	0	4	0	0	0	4	0	0	0	0	0	0	0
Wash.	25	0	1	3	430	32	129	7	21	2	0	4	33	9	5	5	1	22	1	14
Ore.	16	0	3	2	515	35	46	4	12	3	1	3	12	3	4	4	1	3	0	11
Calif.	116	0	5	43	385	185	121	42	274	21	0	58	273	33	52	52	18	112	68	66
U.S.	1,364	1,118	1,232	1,082	6,357	3,163	4,541	715	6,264	2,076	2,582	3,833	4,610	1,158	973	1,552	796	1,174	2,449	1,429

* Source: Department of Commerce, Bureau of the Census, Census of Manufactures: 1954.

Table C-4. Employment in Manufacturing Industries, 1947, as a Percent of Total Employment, 1950, by States

Major industry group

States	Food X'_{41}	Tobacco X'_{42}	Textiles X'_{43}	Apparel X'_{44}	Lumber X'_{45}	Furniture X'_{46}	Paper X'_{47}	Printing X'_{48}	Chemicals X'_{49}	Petroleum & coal X'_{50}	Rubber X'_{51}	Leather X'_{52}	Stone, clay & glass X'_{53}	Primary metals X'_{54}	Fabricated metals X'_{55}	Machinery X'_{56}	Electrical machinery X'_{57}	Transportation equipment X'_{58}	Instruments X'_{59}	All manufacturing X'_{60}
Me.	2.7		8.3	1.1	3.9	0.2	5.3	0.6	0.2	0.0	0.1	5.0	0.2	0.1	0.6	2.1		1.1		32.1
N.H.	0.9	0.2	10.0	1.2	3.2	0.8	2.8	1.2	0.2			9.9	0.5	0.3	0.8	3.1			0.3	36.9
Vt.	1.3	0.0	3.4	1.3	3.9	1.3	1.9	0.8	0.2			0.3	1.9	0.5	0.6	5.2		0.0		25.4
Mass.	2.3		7.0	2.6	0.4	0.6	1.9	1.9	1.0	0.1	1.4	3.9	0.6	1.1	2.2	4.8	3.0	1.0	0.9	39.3
R.I.	1.4		20.5	1.0	0.2	0.3	0.7	1.1	0.4		2.2	0.1	0.3	1.7	2.6	5.7	1.7	0.1	0.6	48.4
Conn.	0.9	0.1	4.7	2.0	0.2	0.3	0.9	1.3	0.9	0.0	1.3	0.2	0.7	4.2	6.8	9.4	4.1	3.6	2.3	48.3
N.Y.	2.2	0.0	1.5	6.4	0.3	0.6	1.1	2.8	1.1	0.1	0.1	1.2	0.7	1.3	1.5	2.3	1.7	1.5	1.5	29.8
N.J.	2.3	0.3	3.2	3.6	0.2	0.4	1.1	1.0	4.2	0.8	0.9	0.5	1.4	2.0	2.2	3.4	4.8	2.3	0.9	37.6
Pa.	2.5	0.5	3.5	3.6	0.4	0.5	0.9	1.4	1.1	0.7	0.4	0.8	1.8	6.7	2.9	3.5	2.4	1.6	0.5	36.7
Ohio	2.0	0.1	0.4	1.0	0.3	0.8	1.0	1.6	1.2	0.4	2.7	0.6	2.0	5.8	4.0	7.4	3.0	3.1	0.3	39.0
Ind.	2.7	0.1	0.4	1.1	0.6	1.4	0.6	1.0	1.3	1.1	1.0	0.2	1.4	5.4	2.7	5.0	3.6	5.3	0.2	36.1
Ill.	3.7	0.0	0.3	1.7	0.4	0.8	0.8	2.6	1.3	0.5	0.1	0.8	0.9	2.8	3.2	6.2	3.7	1.3	0.9	33.4
Mich.	1.8	0.0	0.3	0.4	0.7	0.9	1.1	0.9	1.4	0.1	0.6	0.2	0.9	3.9	3.8	6.3	0.9	15.8	0.2	40.8
Wis.	3.1		0.8	0.7	1.2	0.9	2.1	1.2	0.4	0.1	0.4	1.6	0.7	1.8	2.7	6.9	2.2	2.2	0.4	30.9
Minn.	3.5	0.0	0.4	0.8	0.6	0.2	1.0	1.6	0.4	0.1	0.1	0.1	0.3	0.6	1.0	2.1	0.8	0.3	0.6	15.9
Iowa	4.3			0.4	0.5	0.2	0.1	0.9	0.5		0.2	0.1	0.5	0.3	0.5	3.4	0.5	0.3	0.1	14.0
Mo.	3.1	0.1	0.2	2.4	0.5	0.5	0.6	1.4	1.0	0.2		2.8	0.9	0.9	1.5	1.6	1.1	1.6	0.2	21.5
N.D.	1.1					0.0		0.4	0.0				0.1		0.1	0.0				2.3
S.D.	2.5				0.4			0.5	0.1				0.1		0.0	0.2				4.2
Neb.	4.6			0.2	0.1	0.2	0.2	0.8	0.3	0.0			0.2		0.3	0.5		0.3		9.2
Kan.	3.7			0.3	0.1	0.1	0.2	0.8	0.7	0.6		0.0	0.5	0.2	0.6	0.7	0.4	1.4		10.5

	Del.	Md.	D.C.	Va.	W.Va.	N.C.	S.C.	Ga.	Fla.	Ky.	Tenn.	La.	Miss.	Ark.	La.	Okla.	Tex.	Mont.	Ida.	Wyo.	Colo.	N.M.	Ariz.	Utah	Nev.	Wash.	Ore.	Calif.	U.S.
1	27.4	25.6	4.8	18.8	20.3	26.1	25.0	19.9	7.8	13.6	19.6	20.0	10.8	10.7	15.1	7.4	10.8	7.2	8.2	5.2	11.3	3.2	5.9	10.7	4.2	17.2	18.3	17.0	25.4
2	0.3	0.1	0.0	0.1	0.0	0.0				0.1	0.1	0.0	0.0	0.2	0.0	0.1	0.0				0.1			0.0		0.0		0.2	
3	0.9	3.6		1.4		0.1	0.1	0.3	0.5	0.3	0.4	0.8		0.1	1.1	0.2	0.8	0.0	0.0		0.2	0.1	0.0			2.8	0.5	2.9	
4		1.0	0.0	0.7				0.1	0.0	0.5	0.1			0.0			0.1				0.1			0.0		0.1	0.1	0.5	
5	2.2	1.2	0.1	0.5		0.3	0.2	0.5	0.1	1.1	0.5	0.7	0.1	0.1	0.2	0.8	0.8	0.0	0.2	0.1	0.9	0.0	0.2	0.3		0.6	0.7	1.3	2.8
6	1.7	2.0	0.1	0.5	1.7	0.2	0.0	0.3	0.2	1.2	1.3	0.7	0.1	0.1	0.4	0.5	0.5	0.1	0.0		0.5	0.1	0.2	0.4		0.6	0.7	1.3	1.7
7	2.5	3.5	0.3	3.4		0.1	0.1	0.2	0.0	0.8	1.3	3.8	0.0	0.5	0.1	0.4	0.4	1.6	0.5		1.6			1.4	2.8	1.0	0.5	0.8	2.0
8	0.2	0.8	0.1	0.4	4.8	0.4	0.4	0.6	0.3	0.4	0.7	0.6	0.3	0.4	0.4	0.6	0.4	0.3	0.2	0.3	0.5	0.2	0.4	0.5	0.6	0.4	0.2	0.7	
9	2.4	0.4	0.5	0.3		0.1	0.0	0.2	0.0	0.4	0.9			0.2		0.0	0.1				0.0					0.0	0.1	0.1	
10		0.6		0.1	0.0					0.0	0.6	0.5		0.2	0.0						0.0								
11	0.1	0.3	0.0	0.4				0.0	0.0	0.1	0.1	0.3		0.2	1.4	1.0	1.4	0.3	2.1		0.2	0.0	0.6			0.0	0.1	0.6	
12	5.6	2.0	0.0	2.9	3.3	0.6	0.5	0.9	0.5	0.5	2.5	0.8	0.7	0.7	1.5	0.2	0.8	0.2	0.1	0.0	0.3	0.2	0.2	0.3	0.6	0.2	0.2	0.7	1.1
13	0.7	1.1	2.6	0.5	0.5	0.4	0.3	0.5	0.6	0.6	0.8	0.4	0.2	0.4	0.5	0.7	0.6	0.6	0.5	0.5	1.0	0.6	0.6	0.8	0.6	0.8	0.8	1.1	
14	0.6	0.6	0.2	0.9	0.2	0.5	0.8	0.6	0.6	0.1	0.4	0.6	0.7	0.5	1.6	0.0	0.2				0.1					1.5	0.8	0.3	0.8
15	0.0	0.3	0.1	1.2	0.1	1.9	0.3	0.5	0.2	0.7	0.7	0.2	0.2	0.5	0.2	0.2	0.2	0.0			0.1	0.1	0.1	0.2		0.4	0.6	0.5	
16	1.1	0.5	2.0	1.3		2.1	2.9	2.7	1.6	1.2	1.8	3.6	4.1	4.7	3.3	0.3	1.1	2.1	3.7	0.8	0.5	0.9	1.1	0.3	0.6	5.1	8.9	1.0	
17	2.0	2.6	0.1	1.3	0.6	1.1	1.4	2.0	0.2	1.3	1.7	0.8	1.5	0.4	0.7	0.1	0.8	0.0			0.3	0.1	0.0	0.5		0.3	0.3	1.1	1.9
18	2.2	0.7	2.9	0.6		14.4	16.5	8.2	0.0	0.4	3.2	5.1	0.7		0.3		0.3				0.0			0.2		0.1	0.5	0.1	
19		0.0		1.5	0.2	2.2	0.3		0.9		1.0	0.2		0.1		0.0													
20	4.0	3.6	1.2	1.8	0.9	1.1	1.0	2.1	1.9	2.4	1.8	1.1	1.0	1.5	3.2	1.8	2.0	1.6	2.3	1.2	3.1	0.8	1.3	3.1	0.9	3.0	2.9	3.0	2.4

APPENDIX D

THE CORRELATION MATRICES OF THE INDEPENDENT VARIABLES

Table D-1. Correlation Matrix of the Independent Variables of the Absolute-Growth (Original) Model

	Industry-general variables													Industry-specific variables			
	X_1	X_2	X_3	X_4	X_5	X_6	X_7	X_8	X_9	X_{10}	X_{11}	X_{12}	X_{13}	X_{14}	X_{15}	X_{16}	X_{17}
X_1	1	.71	.45	.51	.60	−.18	.12	.31	.25	.21	.69	.58	.50	na	.50	na	.52
X_2		1	.93	.92	.92	−.21	.16	.32	.05	.35	.98	.96	.91	.73	.88	.80	.80
X_3			1	.95	.91	−.22	.15	.35	.00	.41	.90	.93	.91	.73	.89	.82	.81
X_4				1	.97	−.32	.15	.33	−.02	.41	.88	.89	.91	.77	.94	.90	.92
X_5					1	−.37	.12	.34	−.03	.40	.87	.86	.86	.75	.90	.89	.90
X_6						1	.31	−.17	−.01	−.26	−.18	−.17	−.24	−.38	−.23	−.37	−.34
X_7							1	.23	.27	.10	.19	.18	.23	.14	.27	.16	.19
X_8								1	.66	.73	.30	.25	.36	.30	.36	.37	.42
X_9									1	.36	.08	.02	.09	.03	.10	.06	.10
X_{10}										1	.31	.30	.35	.26	.38	.39	.41
X_{11}											1	.98	.92	.75	.88	.77	.75
X_{12}												1	.89	.68	.89	.74	.71
X_{13}													1	.89	.93	.88	.85

	Industry-specific variables															
	X_{18}	X_{19}	X_{20}	X_{21}	X_{22}	X_{23}	X_{24}	X_{25}	X_{26}	X_{27}	X_{28}	X_{29}	X_{30}	X_{31}	X_{32}	X_{33}
X_1	.48	.47	na	na	na	na	.88	na	.51	.46	.44	.49	na	na	na	.68
X_2	.74	.56	.85	.93	.01	.22	.82	.29	.80	.74	.90	.66	.56	.43	.54	.88
X_3	.78	.55	.85	.87	−.02	.19	.81	.10	.79	.71	.93	.61	.49	.48	.57	.79
X_4	.86	.67	.80	.84	.00	27	.77	.12	.83	.76	.91	.62	.51	.64	.59	.84
X_5	.80	.68	.71	.84	.04	.28	.69	.17	.82	.76	.86	.72	.65	.63	.54	.88
X_6	−.26	−.30	−.09	−.17	−.10	−.12	−.15	.06	−.29	−.09	−.24	−.37	−.23	−.32	−.08	−.31
X_7	.17	.17	.24	.22	−.06	.06	.17	−.14	.08	.15	.11	−.03	.06	.05	.31	.08
X_8	.36	.39	.30	.35	−.22	−.29	.15	.26	.15	.17	.29	.15	.22	.25	.13	.29
X_9	.09	.11	.11	.06	−.29	−.35	−.06	.17	−.15	−.06	−.04	−.15	.02	.07	.08	.04
X_{10}	.37	.32	.27	.43	−.23	−.24	.21	.34	.23	.35	.38	.15	.18	.26	.24	.36
X_{11}	.69	.51	.91	.90	.01	.25	.88	.27	.74	.72	.89	.63	.51	.39	.59	.85
X_{12}	.68	.46	.89	.89	.02	.28	.89	.20	.76	.72	.91	.59	.51	.40	.65	.82
X_{13}	.77	.58	.94	.81	−.06	.23	.87	.09	.71	.69	.88	.60	.39	.49	.62	.77
X_{14-20}*												.61				.77

	Industry-specific variables															
	X_{34}	X_{35}	X_{36}	X_{37}	X_{38}	X_{39}	X_{40}	X_{42}	X_{44}	X_{49}	X_{53}	X_{54}	X_{55}	X_{56}	X_{58}	X_{59}
X_1	na	.77	na	na	.34	na	.60	na	.39	na	.46	.87	na	na	−.48	.26
X_2	.67	.81	.71	.75	.39	.67	.92	.17	.75	.77	.76	.64	.80	.74	.55	.74
X_3	.69	.85	.83	.85	.41	.74	.91	.13	.78	.76	.78	.70	.87	.85	.53	.82
X_4	.80	.93	.87	.85	.52	.66	.97	.19	.72	.80	.85	.81	.95	.92	.64	.75
X_5	.84	.92	.84	.82	.54	.54	1.00	.25	.63	.82	.86	.83	.93	.88	.66	.63
X_6	−.43	−.40	−.33	−.30	−.18	−.03	−.37	−.18	−.09	−.39	−.39	−.42	−.40	−.33	−.22	−.10
X_7	−.02	.10	.10	.18	.11	.17	.12	−.05	.16	.06	−.01	.00	.11	.16	.13	.20
X_8	.31	.39	.34	.30	.33	.19	.34	−.24	.16	.21	.26	.25	.37	.36	.38	.23
X_9	−.03	.05	.04	−.01	.08	.00	−.03	−.31	−.05	−.15	−.07	−.05	.02	.04	.09	.01
X_{10}	.41	.44	.39	.39	.28	.18	.40	−.15	.20	.29	.43	.40	.44	.42	.33	.24
X_{11}	.60	.73	.64	.73	.31	.75	.87	.16	.82	.76	.72	.58	.74	.68	.48	.80
X_{12}	.61	.73	.67	.75	.27	.76	.86	.17	.84	.71	.71	.60	.75	.70	.44	.82
X_{13}	.61	.79	.73	.88	.35	.82	.86	.09	.84	.85	.74	.62	.83	.79	.50	.89
X_{14-20}*	.82	.93	.88		.84	.93				.86	.76	.85	.94	.92	.89	.95
X_{21-40}*								.88	.98	.79	.90	.94	.98	.96	.97	.98

* The correlation coefficients for the various industry-specific variables are reported only between variables related to the same industry, for example, X_{14} (chemistry patents) with X_{29} (expenditures for new plant and equipment in the chemical industry) and X_{15} with X_{33} and X_{16} with X_{34} and so forth.
na—Not available.

Table D-2. Correlation Matrix of the Independent Variables of the Rate-of-Growth (Variant) Model

| | Industry-general variables | | | | | | | | | | | | | Industry-specific variables* | | | | | | | |
	X_1'	X_2'	X_3'	X_4'	X_5'	X_6'	X_7'	X_8'	X_9'	X_{10}'	X_{11}'	X_{12}'	X_{13}'	X_{41}'	X_{44}'	X_{47}'	X_{49}'	X_{54}'	X_{55}'	X_{56}'	X_{60}'
X_1'	1	.27	−.41	.08	.42	.17	−.17	−.08	.41	.20	.45	.63	.06	.05	−.09	−.11	.10	.10	.10	−.05	−.12
X_2'		1	−.22	.47	.47	−.69	.33	−.36	−.13	−.11	−.06	−.15	−.15	−.09	−.58	−.43	−.38	−.32	−.53	−.63	−.72
X_3'			1	.38	.03	−.01	.07	.12	.33	.31	.07	−.11	.18	.26	−.09	−.04	−.08	.14	.16	.29	.02
X_4'				1	.51	−.20	.07	.03	.34	.21	.19	.09	.13	.32	−.34	−.51	−.16	.01	−.10	−.14	−.52
X_5'					1	−.16	−.03	−.33	.22	.06	.18	.24	−.09	.20	−.40	−.36	.11	−.08	−.29	−.43	−.56
X_6'						1	−.55	.21	.30	.13	.21	.41	−.02	.17	.43	.06	.60	.36	.57	.53	.59
X_7'							1	.37	−.19	−.21	.10	−.01	.27	−.01	−.30	.18	−.62	−.60	−.56	−.30	−.44
X_8'								1	.13	.04	.29	.29	.34	.16	.21	.27	−.17	−.07	.14	.39	.27
X_9'									1	.78	.61	.54	.13	.37	.09	−.06	.04	.42	.46	.38	.25
X_{10}'										1	.37	.15	−.03	.27	.09	.02	.06	.49	.41	.32	.24
X_{11}'											1	.72	.40	.36	−.14	.09	−.20	.08	.12	.19	.03
X_{12}'												1	.30	.21	.14	−.07	.04	.05	.13	.11	.05
X_{13}'													1	.40	.07	.02	−.25	−.08	.00	.17	.03

* The asymmetry of the dependent variable series of the rate-of-growth variant—due to the editing of the data—complicated the automatic data processing such that the machines could compute the correlation coefficients between the independent variables for only twelve of the twenty industry-specific variables used (X_{41-90}'), and the capacity of the machine further limited this to eight.

APPENDIX E

Figures: Maps Showing Relocation of Manufacturing

Figures 1–20 show, by states, the number of employees in the various groups of industries more or less than the number who would have been employed if the 1947 market shares had been maintained in 1954. A plus sign signifies an increase and a zero, a decrease in the market share of approximately 0.2 per cent of the total employment of each industry group. The absolute value varies from industry to industry. The data are derived from the U. S. Department of Commerce, Bureau of the Census, *Census of Manufactures, 1947* and *Census of Manufactures, 1954* (Washington, 1950 and 1957).

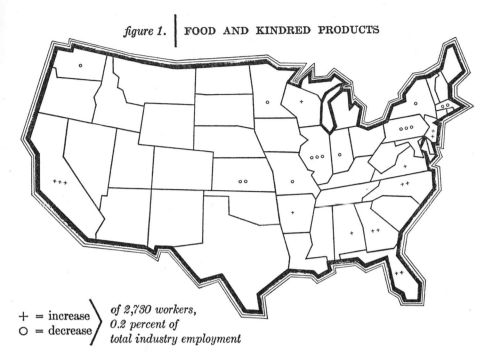

figure 1. | FOOD AND KINDRED PRODUCTS

+ = increase ⟩ of 2,730 workers,
O = decrease ⟩ 0.2 percent of
total industry employment

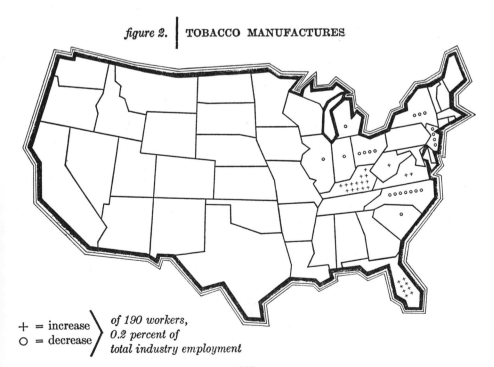

figure 2. | TOBACCO MANUFACTURES

+ = increase ⟩ of 190 workers,
O = decrease ⟩ 0.2 percent of
total industry employment

107

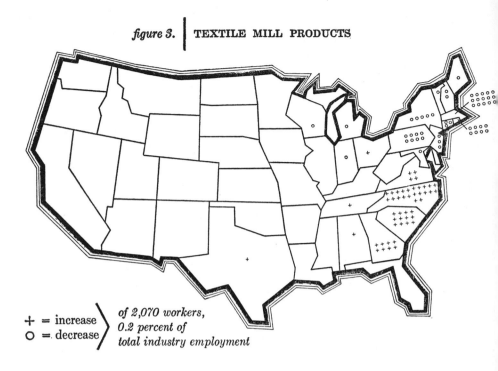

figure 3. | TEXTILE MILL PRODUCTS

+ = increase ⎫
O = decrease ⎭
of 2,070 workers,
0.2 percent of
total industry employment

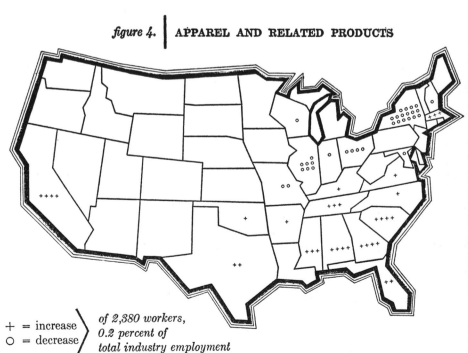

figure 4. | APPAREL AND RELATED PRODUCTS

+ = increase ⎫
O = decrease ⎭
of 2,380 workers,
0.2 percent of
total industry employment

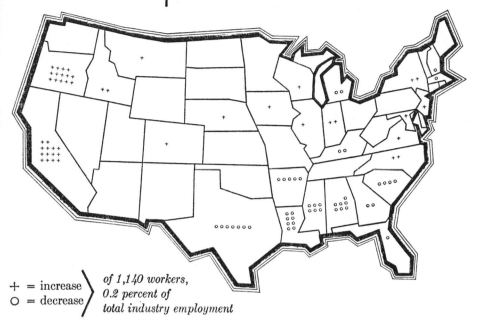

figure 5. | LUMBER AND RELATED PRODUCTS

+ = increase ⎫ of 1,140 workers,
O = decrease ⎬ 0.2 percent of
⎭ total industry employment

figure 6. | FURNITURE AND FIXTURES

+ = increase ⎫ of 680 workers,
O = decrease ⎬ 0.2 percent of
⎭ total industry employment

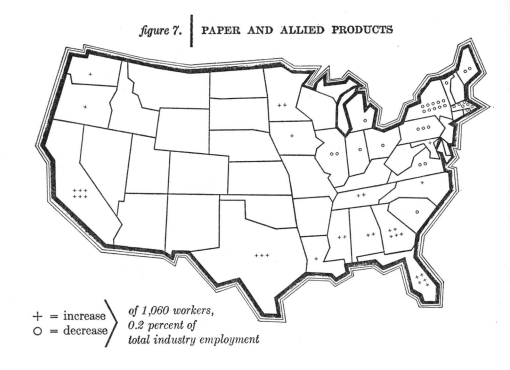

figure 7. | PAPER AND ALLIED PRODUCTS

+ = increase ⟩ of 1,060 workers,
○ = decrease ⟩ 0.2 percent of
total industry employment

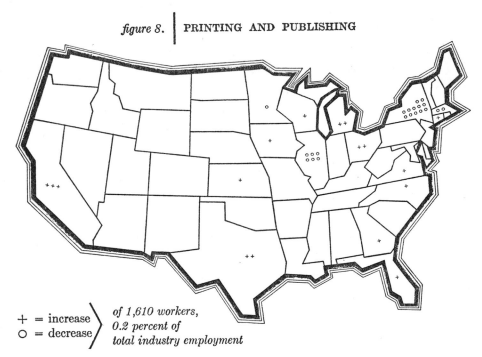

figure 8. | PRINTING AND PUBLISHING

+ = increase ⟩ of 1,610 workers,
○ = decrease ⟩ 0.2 percent of
total industry employment

figure 9. | CHEMICALS AND ALLIED PRODUCTS

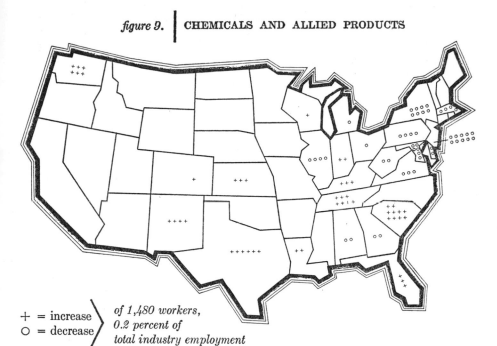

+ = increase ⟩ of 1,480 workers,
O = decrease ⟩ 0.2 percent of
total industry employment

figure 10. | PETROLEUM AND COAL PRODUCTS

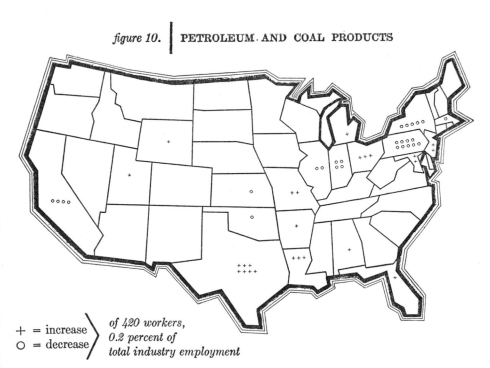

+ = increase ⟩ of 420 workers,
O = decrease ⟩ 0.2 percent of
total industry employment

figure 11. RUBBER PRODUCTS

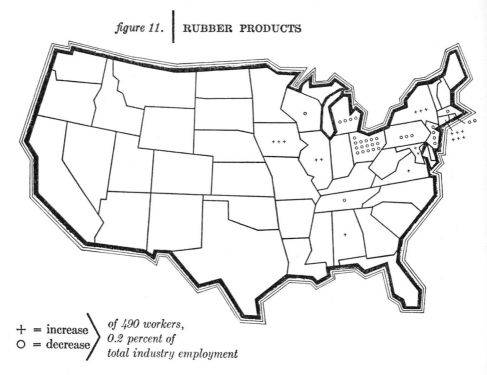

+ = increase ⎫ of 490 workers,
○ = decrease ⎬ 0.2 percent of
        ⎭ total industry employment

figure 12. | LEATHER AND LEATHER PRODUCTS

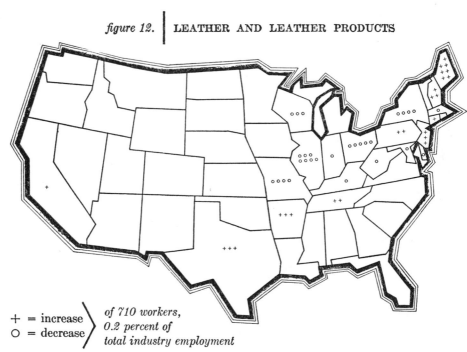

+ = increase ⎫ of 710 workers,
○ = decrease ⎬ 0.2 percent of
        ⎭ total industry employment

112

figure 13. | STONE, CLAY AND GLASS PRODUCTS

+ = increase ⟩ *of 980 workers,*
O = decrease ⟩ *0.2 percent of*
total industry employment

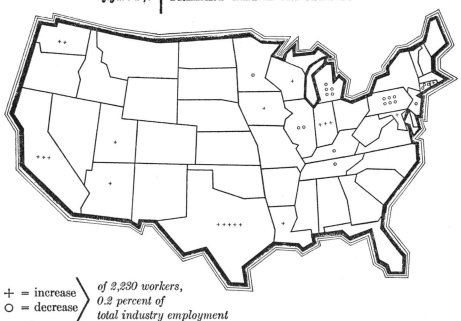

figure 14. | PRIMARY METAL INDUSTRIES

+ = increase ⟩ *of 2,230 workers,*
O = decrease ⟩ *0.2 percent of*
total industry employment

figure 15. | FABRICATED METAL PRODUCTS

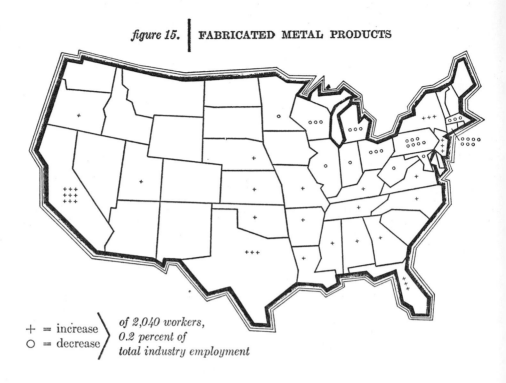

+ = increase ⎰ of 2,040 workers,
○ = decrease ⎱ 0.2 percent of
              total industry employment

figure 16. | MACHINERY, EXCEPT ELECTRICAL

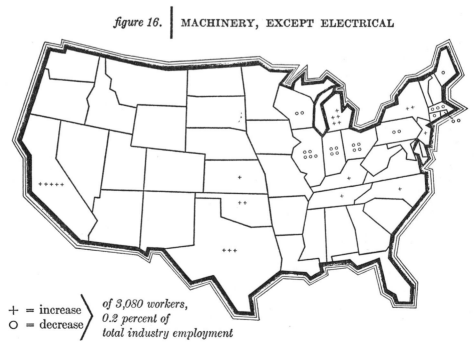

+ = increase ⎰ of 3,080 workers,
○ = decrease ⎱ 0.2 percent of
              total industry employment

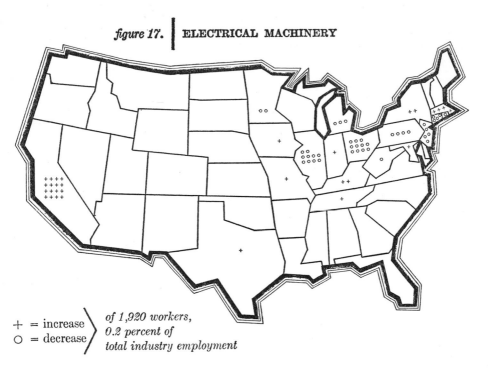

figure 17. | ELECTRICAL MACHINERY

+ = increase ⟩ of 1,920 workers,
○ = decrease ⟩ 0.2 percent of
total industry employment

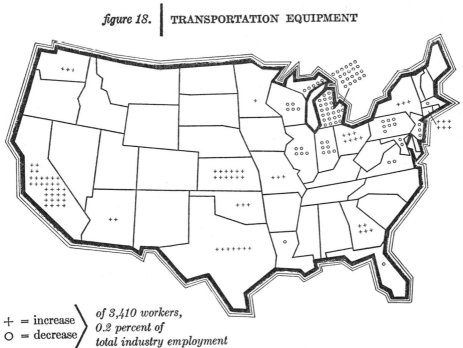

figure 18. | TRANSPORTATION EQUIPMENT

+ = increase ⟩ of 3,410 workers,
○ = decrease ⟩ 0.2 percent of
total industry employment

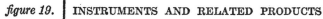

figure 19. | INSTRUMENTS AND RELATED PRODUCTS

+ = increase ⟩ of 540 workers,
○ = decrease ⟩ 0.2 percent of
total industry employment

figure 20. | ALL MANUFACTURING

+ = increase ⟩ of 31,300 workers,
○ = decrease ⟩ 0.2 percent of
total industry employment

Manuscript edited by Alexander Brede

Designed by S. R. Tenenbaum
Set in Monotype Modern No. 8 type face
Printed on Warren's Olde Style Antique Wove paper
Bound in Bancroft's Kennett cloth
MANUFACTURED IN THE UNITED STATES OF AMERICA